Twayne's English Authors Series

Sylvia E. Bowman, *Editor*

INDIANA UNIVERSITY

Compton Mackenzie

 173

Compton Mackenzie

Compton Mackenzie

By D. J. Dooley

St. Michael's College
University of Toronto

Twayne Publishers, Inc.   ::   New York

Library of Congress Cataloging in Publication Data

Dooley, David Joseph, 1921-
  Compton Mackenzie.

  (Twayne's English authors series, TEAS 171)
  1. Mackenzie, Sir Compton, 1883-1972.
PR6025.A2526Z6   828'.9'1209   74-1445
ISBN 0-8057-1361-1

PR
6025
·A2526
Z6

Contents

About the Author

D. J. Dooley, born in Halifax, Nova Scotia, received a B. A. from the University of Western Ontario, an M. A. from the University of Toronto, and a Ph. D. from the University of Iowa. He has taught at Creighton University, St. Francis Xavier University, the Royal Military College of Canada, and St. Michael's College, University of Toronto, where he is now Professor of English and Chairman of the department.

Dr. Dooley has written articles on a wide variety of subjects, from the limitations of George Orwell to the limitations of scientists and Freudian critics. His special interest, however, is in satire and fiction. He has written articles on such writers as Swift, Thackerary, James, and Waugh; a book on *Sinclair Lewis* (Nebraska, 1967); and a pamphlet discussion of *Contemporary Satire* (Toronto, 1971).

Preface

With metaphors oddly mixed, Henry James once described D. H. Lawrence as hanging "in the dusty rear" behind "the boat" of Hugh Walpole, Gilbert Cannan, and Compton Mackenzie. Lawrence's ship has sailed through many turbulent waters since 1914, but it still remains afloat. As to his rivals, the first was hit below the waterline by Somerset Maugham, the second took madness for its pilot and disappeared from view, and the third seemed to roam all over the map with little evidence of the clear sense of direction which a great ship normally manifests. Through all the years, however, that ship kept sailing on; should we not pay tribute to the intrepidity and skill of its navigator?

The early stage of exaggerated critical acclaim for Compton Mackenzie (typified by James's estimate of him[1]) has been followed by almost complete neglect. Ernest Baker's ten-volume *History of the English Novel* names him only once, in a paragraph dealing with Robert Louis Stevenson's rehabilitation of the novel of incident. William York Tindall mentions him twice in his *Forces in Modern British Literature, 1884-1946* — including his *Sinister Street* in a list of novels of adolescence and linking his *Extraordinary Women* with Radclyffe Hall's *The Well of Loneliness* as "unimportant studies of abnormality." G. S. Fraser mentions him once in *The Modern Writer and his World* — but only as an example of Norman Douglas's influence.[2] Arnold Kettle's *Introduction to the English Novel,* Walter Allen's survey of the novel since 1920 in *Tradition and the Dream,* Boris Ford's Penguin volume on twentieth-century English literature, and many similar studies make no reference to him at all. Undoubtedly, the present critical estimate of him as a novelist would approximate Lionel Stevenson's:

Compton Mackenzie displayed a flair for comedy and what seemed to be daring impropriety in *Carnival* (1912) dealing with the theatrical world to which his parents belonged, and *Sinister Street* (1913), based on his experiences at St. Paul's School and Oxford. A more serious ethical outlook was manifested by Hugh Walpole in *The Prelude to Adventure and Fortitude*. Both Mackenzie and Walpole wrote numerous novels through many subsequent years, winning knighthoods as reward for their popular appeal, but neither proved to possess the depth of understanding or the artistic integrity essential for creating great fiction.[3]

But there are signs that this view is being revised. In 1962, Edmund Wilson argued in an interview that Mackenzie was unjustly neglected:

... I'd like to say something about someone I know you're not going to ask me about: the writer that nobody — in London, at least — takes seriously. ... I mean Compton Mackenzie.
He makes a mistake nowadays, I think, in always describing himself as an "entertainer." A good many of his books, actually, since his early period, are meant to convey "a message". ... For years he has been trying to plead in his books for the rights of small nations and cultural minorities, as against all the forces that are driving us in the direction of a centralized power that tries to process or crush them.[4]

In illustration, Wilson pointed out that the long novel *The Four Winds of Love* really amounts to a defense of oppressed and recalcitrant groups, including even the Bretons and the Cornish; but he said that he had never seen a review of one of the later novels which gave any indication of what Mackenzie was driving at.

In Wilson's opinion, obviously, Mackenzie possessed a more serious ethical outlook and a greater degree of artistic integrity than Lionel Stevenson gave him credit for. As Wilson also showed, the reasons for misunderstanding, particularly by English reviewers, were not far to seek:

The trouble is that he is both a professed Scot and something of a crypto-American, so he is always at an angle to English society. They don't understand him or don't want to understand him, and I suppose they resent such a comic portrait as that of Captain Waggett in the Scottish series — which is so lightly done but so deadly in intention — more than anything in Bernard Shaw. And nobody is able to bring himself to give Mackenzie credit for being the fine artist that at his best he is.[5]

There are some signs, however, that the English are beginning to make amends. Discussing the reception of the seventh volume of Mackenzie's autobiography, Walter Allen wrote,

It has been reviewed at greater length and more enthusiastically, I think, than any of the previous volumes — I suspect because we're beginning to wonder whether we've ever done justice to this remarkable man who is part of the history of our time, has known almost everybody worth knowing in his lifetime and is as much at home with men of action as with artists.

We still tend to think of him primarily as the author of "Sinister Street," which was "The Catcher in the Rye" of its generation. But then, among so much else, there are the splendid comic novels of Capri life, "Vestal Fire" and "Extraordinary Women," and, much more recently, that striking study of homosexuality, "Thin Ice." It's time someone attempted a serious assessment of his works.[6]

There is ample justification, therefore, for a study of Mackenzie's long and varied career.

The nineteenth century, Mackenzie wrote, went out in the south of England "to a savage gale, so savage that one of the megaliths of Stonehenge was blown down. . . ; I have always felt this was an omen of how much of the past the twentieth century would destroy."[7] He sometimes described himself as a Jacobite Tory out of the mid-eighteenth century; he also said that he would like to have spent his prime in Periclean Athens or Medicean Florence. But this feeling of alienation from his own time never made him bitter or destroyed his zest for existence: "Having been born when I was, I have tried to make the best of it."[8] In *My Life and Times*, he made it apparent that he thought of his life as full and fortunate — a rare attitude for a twentieth-century novelist.

World War I, which took the lives of so many of his coevals, and soured the outlook of so many others, made Mackenzie the temporary ruler of a chain of Greek islands and gave him the chance to roam over the Aegean sea like one of the heroes of the Homeric Age. In the postwar years, he moved from place to place with all D. H. Lawrence's restlessness, but, unlike Lawrence, always into a congenial environment: his autobiography is a monument to friendships made and kept, and to three happy marriages. He lived to write a hundred books, to receive a knighthood, to be made a Companion of Literature, and to have a special exhibition of his works in the National Library of Scotland on his eighty-fifth birthday. But we have to judge a writer's success by other criteria besides fullness of life, honors and awards.

The source of both Mackenzie's strength and weakness as a novelist was his amazing memory. He once wrote,"I have always felt that one justification for writing my life was the exceptional memory I have of my childhood. So far I have not met anybody who could claim a practically continuous memory of his life from before he was two years old, and not merely of incidents in that life but of what he thought about those incidents at the time."[9] So he could convey the experience of growing up in Kensington or going to Oxford in a very authentic way. He rejected the notion that this power of nearly total recall stifled his creative imagination: "I have sometimes read a half-condescending half-contemptuous allusion by modern critics to the part played by memory in a work of imagination. . . . Such critics forgot (if most of them ever knew) that Mnemosyne was by Zeus the author of the Nine Muses. The mythopoea of Hellas had no doubt of the importance of memory to art."[10]

Nonetheless, Mackenzie's fullness of recollection placed an extra burden on his power of selection — which was not always sufficiently strong to deal with its task. Furthermore, he always thought of his writing as his day-to-day work, and he kept at it whether or not he had something worthwhile to say. The consequence was a vast over-production; as Charles Curran says, "His fecundity makes Ceres, the goddess of plenty, look like Dr. Marie Stopes."[11] His work was so uneven and so variegated that it is almost impossible to categorize him. "The modern critical tendency is all for comparison and classification," writes Sheila Kaye-Smith, "but what are you to do with a man who one year writes a trilogy founded entirely on religious experience, and the next produces a serial for a penny daily."[12]

It is apparent, then, that any study of Mackenzie must first of all attempt to sort out the wheat from the chaff. He was preeminently a novelist, and I shall try to show that some of his novels deserve more serious attention than they are usually given. This is perhaps especially true of the early ones; in the 1920's he seemed to abandon all pretense of being a serious novelist and to settle for being an entertainer. But, as Edmund Wilson warns, his entertainments are sometimes more serious than they appear to be, and his later novels have been consistently misunderstood; we have seen Wilson's tribute to his skill in comic and satiric portraiture — "so lightly done but so deadly in intention."

I intend in this study to present fairly detailed consideration of about thirty novels; the only major ones which I will omit are *The Altar Steps, The Parson's Progress,* and *The Heavenly Ladder,* partly because of lack of space to discuss this religious trilogy as fully as it needs and partly because its major themes emerge in other novels. In Mackenzie's nonfictional writing there is a great deal which is of little consequence, but there are a number of volumes of memoirs which are important, as I shall show. Throughout, my main emphasis is twofold: to show that Mackenzie was a much more serious artist than he is usually given credit for being, and that there is a unifying vision in his work from start to finish.

D. J. DOOLEY

St. Michael's College
University of Toronto

Acknowledgments

The occasions on which I met Sir Compton Mackenzie, in Edinburgh, London, and Pradelles in Central France, were memorable ones for me. Sir Compton is no longer here to thank for his flow of witty conversation, but I can at least thank Lady Mackenzie for her gracious hospitality to me and to my wife. I should also like to express gratitude to Miss Joyce Weiner, Sir Compton's literary agent, for her most useful assistance.

I wish to thank the executors of the estate of the late Sir Compton Mackenzie and Chatto and Windus for permission to quote from the following books by Mackenzie: *Gallipoli Memories, Water on the Brain, The Four Winds of Love, Literature in My Time, The Monarch of the Glen, The Red Tapeworm, Keep the Home Guard,* and *My Life and Times.*

Also George G. Harrap and Company for permission to quote from two books by Mackenzie, *Mr. Roosevelt* and *Dr. Benes;*

John Johnson and Peter Davies, Ltd., for permission to quote from Arthur Swinson's *Scotch on the Rocks;*

T. F. Burns, editor of *The Tablet,* for permission to quote from a review by Derek Traversi; and the Society of Authors, holders of the copyright in Mackenzie's books.

Chronology

1883   Compton Mackenzie born at West Hartlepool, Yorkshire, England, on January 17.

1886   Family moves to 54 Avonmore Road, West Kensington, London.

1891   Enters Colet Court preparatory school.

1894   Enters St. Paul's School.

1901   Enters Magdalen College, Oxford.

1904   With Christopher Stone, buys Ladyham Cottage at Burford in the Cotswolds. Graduates from Oxford with a second in history.

1905   Marries Faith Stone, Christopher's sister.

1907   Play *The Gentleman in Grey* produced; *Poems* published. Moves to Cornwall.

1910   Writes lyrics for H. G. Pélissier's *Follies.*

1911   Publication of first novel, *The Passionate Elopement.*

1912   *Carnival.* Tours United States in dramatic version of *Carnival.*

1913   Moves to Capri. First volume of *Sinister Street.*

1914   Becomes a Roman Catholic. Second volume of *Sinister Street.*

1915   Goes to Gallipoli as lieutenant of Royal Marines. *Guy and Pauline.*

1917   End of military service; returns to Capri.

1918   *The Early Life and Adventures of Sylvia Scarlett.*

1919   *Sylvia and Michael. Poor Relations.*

1920   Leases Herm and Jethou in the Channel Islands. *The Vanity Girl.*

1921   *Rich Relatives.*

1922   *The Altar Steps,* beginning of a religious trilogy. Founds *The Gramophone.*

1923 *The Seven Ages of Woman. The Parson's Progress*, second volume of religious trilogy.

1924 *The Heavenly Ladder*, final volume of religious trilogy. First broadcast for British Broadcasting Corporation. *Santa Claus in Summer*, a story for children. *The Old Man of the Sea.*

1925 *Coral*, a sequel to *Carnival.*

1926 *Fairy Gold.*

1927 *Rogues and Vagabonds. Vestal Fire.*

1928 *Extraordinary Women.* Beginning of involvement with campaign for Scottish Home Rule.

1929 *The Three Couriers. Gallipoli Memories.*

1930 Moves to Scotland.

1931 *First Athenian Memories.* Elected Rector of Glasgow University.

1932 *Prince Charlie.* Publication of *Greek Memories*, causing conviction in 1933 under the Official Secrets Act. Visit to Poland.

1933 *Water on the Brain. Literature in My Time.*

1934 Builds house on Barra in the Outer Hebrides.

1936 *Catholicism and Scotland.*

1937 *Pericles.* Publication of first volume of *The Four Winds of Love.*

1938 *The Windsor Tapestry*, a defense of the Duke of Windsor.

1940 *Aegean Memories.*

1941 *The Red Tapeworm. The Monarch of the Glen.*

1943 *Keep the Home Guard Turning. Mr. Roosevelt.*

1946 *Dr. Benes.* Begins tour of theaters of war for history of the Indian Army in World War II.

1947 *Whisky Galore.*

1949 *Hunting the Fairies.*

1951 *Eastern Epic*, first volume of his history of the Indian Army.

1952 *The Rival Monster.*

1954 *Ben Nevis Goes East.* Knighted.

1956 *Thin Ice.*

1957 *Sublime Tobacco. Rockets Galore.*

1959 *The Lunatic Republic.*

1960 Death of Faith Compton Mackenzie. *Greece in My Life.*

1962 Marriage to Chrissie MacSween. *On Moral Courage.*

1963 January 17, publication of first volume of *My Life and Times.* Death of second wife, Chrissie.

1965 Marriage to Lily MacSween. *The Stolen Soprano.*

1966   *Paper Lives.*
1968   Made a Companion of Literature.
1971   *My Life and Times* completed with publication of tenth volume.
1972   Dies in Edinburgh on November 30.

CHAPTER 1

A Full Life

I *Escaping the Stage*

THE early life of Edward Montague Compton Mackenzie was a long struggle to escape his hereditary calling — the stage. His paternal grandfather had had a distinguished career under the stage name of Henry Compton, and his last London appearance was as First Gravedigger in a *Hamlet* produced by H. L. Bateman, Mackenzie's other grandfather. Bateman was an American; two of his daughters, Kate and Ellen, were touring the United States in scenes from Shakespeare when they were only six and four years old, respectively; and Kate later became one of the leading actresses of her day. A third daughter, Virginia, married Henry Compton's son Edward; both of them being actors, they established the Compton Comedy Company, which toured the British Isles for thirty-five years. Their first son — the one who was to defy his ancestry and become a writer — was born while they were in West Hartlepool, Durham, on January 17, 1883. They continued on tour after he was born: "Every week, except for five weeks in the summer at Lowestoft, a different place and sometimes two different places in the same week. Sunday after Sunday in the train."[1] His incurable wanderlust came naturally to him.

But, as the family grew, his parents saw the necessity of establishing a home for their children; and they bought a house in the London district of West Kensington. The London when John Galsworthy's Forsytes were in their heyday was the London of Mackenzie's youth, and he possessed a remarkably vivid recollection of it. How many writers still active in the Space Age could remember horse-drawn buses, crossing sweepers, and the gas-jet lamps put up for Queen Victoria's Golden Jubilee in 1887? And Mackenzie did not forget his first meeting with a famous novelist whom we have already mentioned: he was taken to see Henry James in 1890 when his father was producing the dramatic version of *The American.*

After several years at Colet Court preparatory school, Mackenzie went to St. Paul's, the great London public school to which John Milton and Samuel Pepys had gone before him. Whether or not he was right when he said that he taught himself to read at the age of two and a half, there is no doubt about his early promise. Professor Norman Bentwich told of being taken around by the headmaster when he first went to St. Paul's and having one boy with tangled hair pointed out to him: "That is Compton Mackenzie. He is the cleverest boy in the school, and will be head of the school in the year 1900."[2] But Mackenzie was never one to satisfy the expectations of headmasters. At Colet Court, his favorite teacher called him a great disappointment, "devoting all his intelligence to inventing various kinds of mischief." At St. Paul's, he objected to being regarded as a prize specimen of academic material, one who would help maintain the school's remarkable record in winning Oxford and Cambridge scholarships. Pedantry repelled him: "I thought the surge and thunder of the Odyssey more important than nice points in Monro's *Homeric Grammar.* I thought the tragedy of that dreadful night when Plataea fell was what mattered in Thucydides much more than Cook's laxatives for the mighty historian's constipated prose."

The thunder of the Odyssey was only a whisper, however, compared to the headmaster's wrath when he found that Mackenzie was not competing for a scholarship at Balliol or Trinity College, Cambridge, or indeed anywhere else — and that he was even going to change from classics to a make-shift history course designed really to accommodate a boy of undoubted promise, G. K. Chesterton, who had floundered about in classics like a beached whale. Mackenzie would never forget the headmaster's oracular denunciation of him: " 'You have been the greatest disappointment to me of any boy who has passed through my hands. You came to St. Paul's a year younger than any boy in the school, already writing Greek iambics many a boy much higher up in the school might have envied. You could have been as great a Greek scholar as Jebb or Porson, and you have flung it all away to swagger up and down the corridors of this school with the manners and appearance of a deboshed clerk.' "[4]

But Mackenzie always maintained that he acted out of a desire to preserve his liberty of thought and action. He was horrified at the mental blinkers his classmates wore, typified by their disputing the merits of the British and Indian Civil Service pension plans: " 'Pensions!' I gasped to myself. 'Pensions. With the world before them they're thinking of their pensions!' " His own world was never so circumscribed — and it was certainly not bounded by school. By age seventeen, he had spent a summer in Britanny; undergone a religious conversion; assisted in stirring up a crisis in the Church of England by helping a boy with High-Church leanings to escape from the home of his Low-Church father; met some of the leading *fin-de-siècle* decadents, especially Lord Alfred Douglas and Reggie Turner; become a passionate Jacobite, expecting the eventual restoration of the Stuarts and meanwhile busying himself with the Carlist restoration in Spain; won commendation from *The Stage* for playing Shylock with "nervous restraint" in a charity production of *The Merchant of Venice;* and, finally, played the part of a sufferer from a nervous breakdown convincingly enough to deceive such knowledgeable drama critics as his father and his mother and win his release from school.

In 1901, Mackenzie entered Magdalen College, Oxford; his experiences there were the basis for what Mortimer R. Proctor, in his study of the university novel, calls "in almost every way the best" of this class of fiction.[5] At the university, he was known for his good looks, flamboyant dress, and extraordinary versatility; the president of his college, rebuking him for neglect of academic work in his third year, listed a formidable number of extracurricular activities — including the founding and editing of a review called *The Oxford Point of View.* When the student paper *Isis* chose him for its 259th Idol (immediately after a future Archbishop of Canterbury), it said that, if he could ever find time to devote more than five minutes to a new idea, the results would be striking. It referred to his literary work, "feverishly committed to paper in crepuscular handwriting," and it made a prescient observation about his seeming at once strikingly old and startlingly young. Three decades later, Ronald Knox would write, "Why I appreciate Compton Mackenzie, and recommend him to the appreciation of others, is that he remains so young, the sort of man professors shake their heads over."[6]

Mackenzie was now thinking of the church and of the law as professions, and trying to escape the stage. After seeing him play Gratiano in *The Merchant of Venice,* the manager of the Garrick Theatre, Arthur Bourchier, offered him a seven-year contract at an excellent salary, after which, he said, Mackenzie would be in a position to make his own terms: "Then the theatre is yours. . . . " Since Mackenzie had now become engaged to the daughter of the bursar of

Worcester College, it seemed willful perversity for him to reject such an opportunity. But his fiancée had a deadly rival, literature; he rejected Bourchier's offer and also a chance for a job on *The Spectator;* instead Mackenzie and his friend Christopher Stone carried out the wildly impractical scheme of buying a cottage in the Cotswolds. The American essayist Logan Pearsall Smith, then living at Oxford, had helped convince Mackenzie that writing was his proper sphere and that he would need a period of semimonastic withdrawal as a preparation for it. He moved to his retreat, curiously, before his final examinations; despite this fact and his previous neglect of his studies, he graduated with a good second-class degree. Not surprisingly, however, his engagement was soon broken.

At this time, Mackenzie thought of himself as essentially a poet; and one of his projects was a blank-verse drama on Joan of Arc. His first book was a volume of poems, brought out at his expense by Blackwell's. Even before it had appeared, he was dissatisfied with it; he had realized that it was too late in the day for its pre-Raphaelite sentiments. The reviewers and his friends also convinced him that he had nothing much to say; he was merely fancying himself inspired by life, when he was really inspired by literature. So he turned from poetry to a comedy in the eighteenth-century manner for his father. Entitled *The Gentleman in Grey,* the play was the product of Mackenzie's close familiarity with the novels and plays of the Augustan Age; the dialogue was second nature to him. The play, first performed in Edinburgh in 1907 soon after its author's twenty-fourth birthday, was successful enough to remain in the repertory of the Compton Comedy Company for several years.

But Mackenzie was dissatisfied with it: "it was not the play as I had seen it in my own mind. I began to ask myself if I was not too good an actor to be a good playwright. Was I going to write plays in the future of which the only good performance from my point of view would be when I read it to the company?"[7] Having disqualified himself as poet and dramatist, he turned with relief to the novel: "I remember the sense of freedom at escaping from the thrall of narrative verse into narrative prose, and the elation of writing dialogue that no actor would have to speak and in speaking destroy that dialogue as I heard it being spoken in my head."[8]

Meanwhile, Mackenzie had left his monastic retreat in the Cotswolds for a more bohemian life in London — and, almost on impulse, had acquired a wife, Christopher Stone's sister Faith. A conversation between Mackenzie and his brother one Thursday morning reveals how impulsive the marriage was:

"Are you doing anything at one o'clock, Frank?"
"No. Why?"
"Well, I'm getting married at one o'clock and I want you to be a witness."⁹

He was still in a mood of tangled uncertainty about his career, and again thinking of ordination as a possibility. For a year he was a lay reader in Cornwall, operating a Sunday School according to unorthodox but highly successful methods. At the same time, he finished turning his play into a novel, first called *Curtain Wells* and later *The Passionate Elopement* (1911). But no one would publish it, and he turned to another occupation: "When that first novel of mine was being refused by publisher after publisher I had taken to growing flowers, determined not to write another novel until that rejected work was accepted and published. If it had never been published I should have been perfectly happy in concentrating the whole of my creative energy on flowers."¹⁰

The alternative careers eliminated themselves: he decided that his lay readership would not be followed by the ministry, and the daffodil fly put an end to his attempt to be a professional gardener. But the stage loomed in front of him once more: his father, who had been giving him an allowance, observed that there was very little evidence that he was ever going to be a successful novelist and asked him to take a part in a new play by Hall Caine. The play, fortunately, lasted only a week; and by the end of that time, *The Passionate Elopement* had been accepted. Martin Secker, as a publisher's reader, had given a favorable report on it; but his recommendation had been overruled by his employer's mistress; when he set up his own publishing firm, it was one of the first books he thought of. Mackenzie was lucky enough to hitch his fortune to a rising star, for Secker was soon to make a reputation as a discoverer of promising novelists.

The novel was published on January 17, 1911, Mackenzie's twenty-eighth birthday; within three weeks, it had to be reprinted; and, by the end of the year, it had gone through four editions. Then Mackenzie had still another stroke of luck. He knew that it was imperative for him to write a second novel as soon as possible, and he had the fortunate experience of conceiving the whole plot of a long novel almost instantaneously. This one, *Carnival,* as Frank Swinnerton says, ran away with the British public. Over the years, it has sold half a million copies; has been produced in dramatic form in both England and the United States; and has been made into a silent and a talking film, and a radio play, and an opera. When Mackenzie began to write a third novel, he intended to tell the story of a public-school boy to compete with that of the youth of lower-class upbringing which H. G. Wells had made popular. This novel was *Sinister Street;* it too sold well, but it also brought Mackenzie serious critical attention — as James's discussion of it indicates, it immediately put Mackenzie in the forefront of living English novelists.

II *Italy and the War*

While Mackenzie was in the United States at the end of 1912 (for a stage production of *Carnival* in which he himself acted), he became severely ill with sciatica — an ailment which tormented him for years. In search of a warmer climate, he and his wife went to Southern Italy. They had already met Norman Douglas and been bewitched by his *Siren Land;* they were equally bewitched by his favorite island as soon as they set foot on it: "The moment we emerged from the funicular in the Piazza we felt that nothing must prevent our living on Capri." So they made their home there in a house called Casa Solitaria, perched high on a cliff. Mackenzie found Capri life as fascinating as Douglas did; and, like him, he put some of its more eccentric human specimens into fiction — but not until some years after he had left it.

Meanwhile, something else happened to him on Capri which illustrates his penchant for going his own way; without in any way condemning the abnormality and immorality he saw around him, and without breaking with Douglas — a notorious scoffer at "upstairs gods" — he was received into the Catholic Church in April, 1914. According to Mackenzie's account, the parocco or parish priest had no need to instruct him in Catholic doctrine; rather, he instructed the parocco — in the mysteries of Anglicanism, High, Low, and Broad Church varieties, which the parocco found thoroughly bewildering. When the war began a few months later, Mackenzie had to intrigue to get into it. After he had had several rebuffs, he heard from a friend on the staff of General Ian Hamilton (the Allied commander in the Dardanelles campaign) that he had caught the general at a propitious moment (namely while reading *Sinister Street)* and had won the promise of a job for Mackenzie. In *Gallipoli Memories* (1929), Mackenzie gives a very moving account of his last look at Capri as he sailed away for the Eastern Mediterranean; "these hours . . . when I look back at them," he writes, "mark like a deep gorge the end of a period of my life."[11]

After a period of dodging shells on the Gallipoli Peninsula, Mackenzie went to Athens to do intelligence work. The situation there was complicated and intriguing: Greece had not yet entered the war, King Constantine was bound to the German side by ties of blood and friendship, and Venizelos, who was in and out of the office of prime minister, strongly favored the Allied side. With considerable zest, Mackenzie entered into the work of interviewing secret agents, conspiring with Venizelist officers and politicians, and doing such other incidental tasks as running counterespionage for the Serbians. Most of the time, he was not carrying out any policy but his own; that of Britain seemed to him an insensate muddle. He attracted sufficient attention to have his house ransacked by Greek reservists in December, 1916; not finding him, they contented themselves with destroying his clothing and the manuscript of a novel. Soon after this episode, he was sent from Athens to occupy the Cyclades Islands in the name of a provisional government which Venizelos had established at Salonika. From commodious headquarters on the island of Syra, he effectively ruled over this part of the Mediterranean; in his own yacht, he visited places whose names had held enchantment for him ever since his days at St. Paul's. Illness and bureaucracy caught up with him, however; by the end of 1917, he was at home on sick leave, working on a novel called *Sylvia Scarlett.*

How had the war influenced his writing? F. Scott Fitzgerald, who visited him on Capri, described him as wrecked by the war, like all the others of his generation.[12] In a second Sylvia Scarlett story, *Sylvia and Michael* (published in the spring of 1919), war-weariness and disgust were very much in evidence. But the war had not left Mackenzie feeble of purpose or devoid of ambition; on the contrary, he began elaborating extremely grandiose schemes. One was for a long series of books, employing the characters in his recent novels, to be called "The Theatre of Youth"; another was for a very long novel about the war to be called "The Chronicles of Argos." The "Chronicles" became *The Labyrinth,* planned in seven volumes; but, after he had settled on the individual titles, he decided it was too soon to write about the war and turned to the composition of a comic novel, *Poor Relations.*

Perhaps this book was the major turning point in his career. Harper's, his American publishers, took a very unfavorable view of the manuscript: "These chapters are no more like Mackenzie than they are like any one of a number of second-grade English and American writers. . . . The writing is commonplace and the reading is dull. . . . The critics will flay the author and the public won't buy the book."[13] Triumphantly Mackenzie records that the book sold thirty-thousand copies within three months and that there was not a single bad review. But, as Theodore Erlandson points out, the reception of the book involved a reestimation of Mackenzie's importance: "a novel of light-hearted humor could not be thought a really suitable venture for a writer for whom such high claims had been made."[14] For example, Douglas Goldring wrote, "Mr. Mackenzie has found himself — not as a serious novelist, but as that very valuable thing, an entertainer."[15]

III   *Mackenzie's Later Career: Fifty Years an Entertainer*

Mackenzie relates that, just before his thirty-sixth birthday, he got a splendid offer from Cassell's: "Six books at £1,500 advance for each and £4,000 option on four of the six for possible serialization. I knew this would be a blow to Martin Secker, but in my financial state I could not refuse such an offer."[16] This bonanza did not solve his financial difficulties; he was in a maze for years, he had to write to keep going, and the more he wrote the worse off he became. In his memoirs, he contrasts himself with Somerset Maugham, who became a millionaire, largely through shrewd investments; he himself never bought a stock in his life, he was a compulsive spender, and, when he was in trouble, his first impulse was to go and buy something.

His favorite type of purchase, curiously, was an island, With D. H. Lawrence, who came to Capri at his invitation, he planned a trip to the South Seas, and perhaps the recolonization of the Kermadec Islands from which the population had been driven by volcanic eruptions. Martin Secker, opposing the South Sea venture as strongly as he could, showed him an advertisement offering the lease of two small Channel islands, Herm and Jethou, and Mackenzie put in a successful application for them. Five years later he bought the Shiant Islands in the Outer Hebrides. It was not without reason then that Lawrence chose the title "The Man Who Loved Islands" for a short story dealing with Mackenzie.[17]

Of course, Mackenzie had badly overestimated his financial capabilities. Building and maintaining a home on Herm proved utterly beyond him, and he had to lease it and move to Jethou, a really small island about a mile in circumference. Lawrence implies in his story that the man who loves islands loves isolation, but Mackenzie had a right to be depressed, on Jethou, when he saw twenty-nine people standing in line on payday — all depending on his literary earnings. His efforts were prodigious:

> I finished *The Old Men of the Sea* toward the end of March and started immediately to write a book for children called *Santa Claus in Summer*. . . .
> The moment I had finished *Santa Claus in Summer* in May I started *The Parson's Progress*.[18]

In a seven-year period ending in December, 1930, he wrote fourteen books; yet he was worse off financially in 1930 than he had been in 1923. His account of these years in *My Life and Times* shows him never free from worry over money matters, and the same worries persisted throughout the 1930's. He writes to his agent in 1936, for example, "I have fended off the Income Tax people with post-dated cheques, but I *must* have enough ready money to keep my household going or I shall crash."[19]

Long before that he had listened to some of his ancestral voices and moved to Scotland, where he soon became identified with the cause of Scottish nationalism. One result was his election to the post of Rector of Glasgow University in 1931; his rectorial address is a notable statement of his opposition to metropolitan and centralizing influences. The 1920's had seen the production of a number of novels of considerable merit but no real distinction; *Vestal Fire* (1927) and *Extraordinary Women* (1928), both set on Capri, were two of the more notable. The same decade had also seen him making a start on his war memoirs; his indiscreet use of classified material in the third volume of these, *Greek Memories,* resulted in his being prosecuted and convicted under the Official Secrets Act in 1933. Out of the experience came a marvelous satire on the intelligence service, *Water on the Brain,* but the trial meant a great deal of strain for Mackenzie, as well as heavy legal expenses.

The financial loss was particularly distressing because he was now trying to get clear time, free from the churning out of potboilers, for what he thought of as his *magnum opus, The Four Winds of Love.* When he began *The Four Winds,* it outgrew its original dimensions with disastrous speed; two volumes appeared in 1937, but they were only the first of six. And, unfortunately, he interrupted work on it to write a long defense of the Duke of Windsor after the abdication crisis, *The Windsor Tapestry*. As a consequence, *The Four Winds* was overtaken by the war; the third volume came in 1940; the last, only in 1945. The work certainly suffered by appearing over an eight-year period, and his great hopes for it were never realized. Meanwhile, he had begun writing about the Scottish scene in shorter novels, such as *The Monarch of the Glen* (1941); the best-known of these is *Whiskey Galore* (1947), out of which a highly successful film was made in which Mackenzie's voice was heard speaking the prologue and epilogue.

When the war ended he was over sixty, and be might have been expected to start slowing down. Instead, he accepted the invitation of the Indian Government to write a history of the Indian Army in World War II, and for this project he made a fifty-thousand-mile tour of every battlefield on which the Indian Army had fought. His willingness to turn to new subjects was shown by such works as the previously mentioned study of homosexuality, *Thin Ice* (1956); by his very amusing satire on a proposal to establish a rocket range in the Hebrides, *Rockets Galore* (1957); and by his individualistic treatment of voyages to the moon in *The Lunatic Republic* (1959). Thinking of himself as a professional writer, who ought normally to be working at his craft, Mackenzie turned his hand to many things besides novels and memoirs. There are studies of Classical Greece, such as a life of Pericles and an account of Marathon and Salamis; a number of books on Scotland, especially on the Stuarts; innumerable children's stories, of which *Santa Claus in Summer* is a classic; and such other miscellaneous writings as *Literature in My Time, On Moral Courage,* and *Sublime Tobacco.* As if the making of many books were not enough to keep him busy, in 1923 he founded *The Gramophone,* an English musical periodical which is still popular; he wrote almost the entire first issue by himself, and continued to contribute to it regularly, writing for example a quarterly six-thousand-word review of records.

Because of *The Gramophone,* he became the first disc jockey, as he whimsically put it: one June day in 1924, he made his first broadcast, playing records and, rather to the horror of the producer, dispensing with a script and making his own *ad lib* comments about them. Subsequently, he was asked to do a regular program; but, since he was living on Jethou, he recommended his brother-in-law, Christopher Stone, who became a famous radio personality. But Mackenzie did not lose his connection with radio; the *Radio Times* said in November, 1966: "Radio drama owes a considerable debt to

Sir Compton Mackenzie. There must . . . still be a good many listeners who will remember the first production of the adaptation by Eric Maschwitz of the famous novel *Carnival* in 1929; it was something of a milestone in the history of the broadcast play. It ran for two hours and a quarter — at a time when the theory flourished that no one would endure listening to any play for more than half an hour."[20] Mackenzie did not prepare the script himself, but he selected the songs for the production, suggested some of the special sound effects, and read the narrative linking the scenes. Over the years he made many broadcasts; and, when television came along, he soon began making appearances on it. It was perhaps as a tribute to the variety of his accomplishments, rather than to his success as a novelist, that he was given a knighthood in 1952. Whatever our final judgment on his books may be, he certainly led a remarkable life.

The crowning achievement of his later years was his autobiography, a remarkable feat of nostalgic memory. With characteristic intrepidity, he planned it in ten volumes; and one volume was to appear annually on his birthday — even though he began it at the age of seventy-eight. In spite of failing vision, he kept up to schedule; and the last volume appeared in January, 1971. By that time, he was almost totally blind; yet all the books in his head were not down on paper; and, as he approached his ninetieth birthday, he was still writing, using a sketch board with wires strung across it to guide his pen. He died in Edinburgh on November 30, 1972.

CHAPTER 2

Knocking at the Door

I   The Passionate Elopement

EVEN though Mackenzie had published only two and a half novels by the time Henry James acclaimed him in "The Younger Generation," James ignored one of them — *The Passionate Elopement.* In his excellent recent estimate of Mackenzie, Kenneth Young gives this novel equally cavalier treatment, merely referring to it as "a period romance," and as "the first of some forty novels."[1] Mackenzie often expressed the opinion that the writer who begins with an autobiographical novel is not likely to make a career of being a novelist.[2] But he himself seemed to have the ill luck, as Reginald Auberon observed, of making a false start in a bastard romanticism.[3] The very appearance of the book emphasized its remoteness from contemporary life: its light blue cloth and gilt lettering gave it an antique elegance; and its deep black print, wide margins, lashing of the *c* and the *t,* use of catch-words at the ends of pages, and archaic spellings such as *heroick* and *mirrour* gave it a period flavor. Could one take seriously a novel published in this way, especially when its characters were frankly referred to as marionettes, porcelain shepherdesses or china dolls, and given names like Beau Ripple, the Earl of Squall, and My Lady Bunbutter?

Leo Robertson, however, calls it "as fine an essay in literary *bravura* as one can find in our literature."[4] He points out that its success with the public was instantaneous and that it received glowing notices from such distinguished periodicals as the *English Review.* In his detailed analysis of the novel, T. R. Erlandson shows that the reviewers had good reasons for not dismissing the novel as trivial; in fact, he makes a better case for it than one would have thought possible.[5] It is frankly a *tour de force,* an exercise in pastiche, yet Erlandson shows that it is intelligently and subtly handled.

The setting is Curtain Wells, which closely resembles Bath and is ruled over by an *arbiter elegantiarum,* Beau Ripple, just as Bath was ruled by Beau Nash for several decades of the eighteenth century. (Mackenzie says that he "had a copy of Anstey's enchanting satire in verse, *The New Bath Guide,* which was of inestimable service for evoking the atmosphere of the imaginary spa called Curtain Wells.")[6] Having conjured up this atmosphere, Mackenzie tells a triangular love story, dealing with the rivalry of Charles Lovely and a disreputable gambler named Francis Vernon for seventeen-year-old Phyllida Courteen. Through deception, Vernon persuades Phyllida to elope with him — and to extract her very valuable pearls from her mother's jewel case. They are pursued and caught, the hero fights a duel with the villain, and obviously enough the hero has to win: he deals a mortal blow to his antagonist. But, ironically, the villain had repented during the chase; won over by Phyllida's charms, he had resolved to marry her honourably:

"Oh, God!" she screamed. "He's dead. Oh! Oh! Oh!"
That anguished cry wounded Lovely deeper than any leaden bullet, for it killed his hopes.[7]

So hero and heroine do not fly into each other's arms; Fortune has made a fool of him, and he resigns himself to bachelorhood. In time, he succeeds Beau Ripple as King of the Wells; he becomes Beau Lovely, and "the indiscretions of his past in course of time acquired a romantick mystery of their own."[8]

In such a costume drama, wrote Douglas Goldring, there was no need for a serious attempt at psychology of characterization.[9] Many of the characters are familiar types, whose interest often lies in the literary echoes which accompany them — and to which Mackenzie sometimes calls attention.[10] In a chapter on "The Confidante," for example, he reflects on this time-honored device which has helped a thousand perplexed authors to unfold their dramas; and he cites examples from Richard Brinsley Sheridan, Tobias Smollett, and Oliver Goldsmith. Since he uses stock figures, views them frankly as puppets, and gives them names emphasizing their unreality — Crumpett the confectioner, Filigree the goldsmith — Mackenzie could hardly have expected them to be taken as real. Yet the settings are convincing. The reviewers, Erlandson says, commented very favorably on the evocation of the manners and atmosphere of the eighteenth century — the effortless and unpedantic depiction of routs and masquerades, cockfights and quadrilles, in a fashionable Augustan watering place. The dialogue also seems particularly successful; it has the ring of spoken language, at least as we know it from eighteenth-century novels and plays. It ranges from the studied elegance of Beau Ripple to the rough talk of innkeepers and serving maids — and these from different shires, as their dialects make clear.[12] Consequently, even though Mackenzie emphasizes the unreality of the characters, the realistic detail and the naturalness of the dialogue make them vivid enough for his purposes.

Erlandson also shows that the plot is carefully structured. It begins on St. Valentine's Day and ends on April Fool's; the dates, of course, parallel the action. The chapters near the beginning are carefully elaborated set pieces, with titles like "The Toilet," "The Pump Room," "The Blue Boar," and so on. Then there is a gradual progression in tempo until the elopement, the chase, and the duel at the end. The one unsure touch, perhaps, is the conclusion, which the London *Daily News* called "one of those pretty pieces of sentimentality to which Stevenson was inclined when he found it necessary to send a villain into the next world. Like the scissors duel in 'St. Ives,' it gives us a blackguard on the edge of death redeemed by a fine attitude."[13] Vernon opens his dark eyes at the touch of his dear one, and gives her a bunch of primroses: "And so with thoughts of flowers, Mr. Francis Vernon died. Pray let that sentence be his epitaph."[14]

The passage may also recall the "poetic beauty" of Julien Sorel's head at the moment when it was about to fall in *Le Rouge et le Noir* (though Mackenzie's great enthusiasm for Stendhal came later, when he read *La Chartreuse de Parme* in 1917).[15] Still another influence is that of Thomas Hardy. The fatal duel occurs, for example, because of a circumstantial irony: Phyllida is asleep in a carriage all the while Charles and Vernon make their preparations. Furthermore, the stage is as melodramatically set as the Stonehenge scene in *Tess of the D'Urbervilles:* Phyllida wakens just in time to see three figures silhouetted against the sky and to watch the fateful duel: "There were two shots, the scud of frightened rabbits to their burrows, a cloud across the sun, a mist over life, and she was kneeling in the dewy grass beside Amor."[16]

Could Mackenzie have made a stranger beginning than with such an artificial and derivative novel? Yet it is dextrously done, and moreover, as Erlandson convincingly argues, it is not so different from Mackenzie's later novels as it is usually considered to be. Erlandson gives an extensive list of similarities: the bias for the sentimental, the descriptive, the melodramatic; the concern for beauty and distinction of style; the realistically effective dialogue and facility of comic invention. Especially noteworthy is the fact that there is a characteristic moral: "Essentially it is a belief in the inherent sacredness of the human personality and the necessity for freedom from external interference if the individual is to fulfill himself. . . . "[17] As he walks away from the duel, Charles Lovely says bitterly, "What right had I to interfere between lovers?" Beau Ripple draws the lesson most emphatically: "My lords, ladies and gentlemen, never meddle with other people's business when it happens to concern the heart or the soul of a human creature. . . . My lords, ladies and gentlemen, you are one and all the genteelest of companions, but so far as my theology has taken me, you are none of you gods and goddesses. . . ."[18]

Erlandson is right in stressing the importance of this principle in Mackenzie's thought. In *More than I Should,* for example, Faith Compton Mackenzie shows how her husband's advocacy of Scottish nationalism was based on a similar attitude: "His enthusiasm for the cause was an earnest of his loathing of standardisation, his deep sense of individualism, of the integrity of small nations. It was the first principle . . . of his life from earliest days."[19] Our desire that others should conform to our own way of life, our suspicion of the anomalous and eccentric and independent — these were Mackenzie's targets from the beginning of his career.

II *Mackenzie's Early Style*

Even if there is a seriously intended moral in *The Passionate Elopement,* does Mackenzie's early style reflect a *fin-de-siècle* sensibility? Erlandson writes, "The chief influences in the formation of Mackenzie's style were, perhaps, George Meredith and, more importantly, the exponents of English and French aestheticism."[20] In *My Life and Times,* Mackenzie quotes some extracts from an article which he wrote for *The Oxford Point of View* in 1903 when he was twenty. Called "The Undergraduate's Garden," it was inspired by Xavier de Maistre's *Voyage autour de ma chambre* and influenced as well by Walter Pater: "A bedroom should be the body's hermitage. . . . The masculine bedroom should contain properly no more than a bed, a bath, and a window open to receive the invigorating currents of fresh air; yet I am prepared to concede to the luxurious an unvarnished washstand, even a dressing-table, on the definite understanding that it should never be used as a beach to gather and to garner the flotsam and jetsam of the day's idleness and the day's work."[21]

As "to gather and to garner" signals, the pretense of high-minded austerity is not matched by austerity in the prose; reading on, we find that the style becomes very ornate: "this hearth, round which in post-prandial security you coin apparelled paradox and postulate un-challenged aphorism. . . . " There are references to François Coppée as well as de Maistre, to François Villon, to Gérard de Nerval. Like Pater, the writer is stirred to reflection by artistic objects, such as the *Mona Lisa:* "Few would wish to refuse La Gioconda the place of honour; she 'upon whose head all the ends of the world are come', may appropriately sit enthroned on the chimney shelf with her elusive smile." "Opposite my desk," he continues, "hangs *Primavera.* Every time I look at it an exquisite emotion thrills me — more intangible than the generality of emotions. I know nothing comparable to it except the feeling I have when I read the first few stanzas of St. Agnes' Eve."

On reading this, we see that the sources are chiefly literary, that the prose is striving and indeed straining for effect, that Mackenzie has no ordinary style of his own to convey his experiences (or the experiences which his reading has taught him that he ought to have). He carries on with pastiche and pretense: "Beware of electric light: it is the symbol of Modernity. Beware, too, of gas; it is a bastard symbol of Modernity, and moreover has a pestilential odour as from some cauldron brewed in a witch's kitchen." Perhaps there is no great significance to such a mannered style; we might expect an undergraduate to parade references to his reading and reflect fashionable attitudes. Nevertheless, the passage shows some of the influences on Mackenzie and the prose style he considers sophisticated at this time.

In *Enemies of Promise* Cyril Connolly praises E. M. Forster for his unpretentious style: "Much of his art consists in the plainness of his writing for he is certain of the truth of his convictions and the force of his emotions. It is the writer who is not so sure what to say or how he feels who is apt to overwrite either to conceal his ignorance or to come unexpectedly on an answer. Similarly it is the novelist who finds it hard to create character who indulges in fine writing."[22] Anyone who has ever tried to analyze the water imagery in *Howards End* might register mild surprise at this reference to Forster's plain style; nevertheless, Connolly gives a good description of overwriting and its causes. He traces back to Addison a style which he christens the Mandarin, "since it is beloved by literary pundits, by those who would make the written word as unlike as possible to the spoken one. It is the style of all those writers whose tendency is to make their language convey more than they mean or more than they feel. . . . "[23]

Among recent examples of it Connolly cites a passage from *The Passionate Elopement* which Sir Arthur Quiller-Couch had included in his *Oxford Book of English Prose,* the description of the *Basket of Roses* inn. After quoting part of it, Connolly observes, "Heigh ho! Georgian prose! Notice the words, especially the adverbs which do not aid but weaken the description, serving only to preserve the architecture of the sentence. [Examples are *plainly perceive, readily recall, haply see.*] They are Addison's legacy. A catalogue of flowers follows. I will begin at flower thirty-five: 'There was Venus' Looking-glass and Flower of Bristol, and Apple of Love and Blue Helmets and Herb Paris. . . . ' "[24] Following this Connolly cites a passage from Rupert Brooke and comments, " 'England has declared war,' he says to himself, 'what had Rupert Brooke better feel about it?' " The reader of Mackenzie can similarly sense his author saying, "Let me now surrender to thoughts of romance. Hand me my Keats and my gold-tooled commonplace book of Arcane Expressions." In a costume drama such as *The Passionate Elopement,* the purple patches are not entirely out of place; in more realistic novels, they sometimes grate. And they can be found in late novels as well as early ones.

Yet when Connolly goes on to say, "the idiom of our time is journalistic and the secret of journalism is to write the way people talk. The best journalism is the conversation of a great talker," he reminds us of the fact that Mackenzie has been both a journalist and a great talker. It would have been almost impossible for a writer to have written as many books as Mackenzie if he had used only High Mandarin. Whether or not he began as a disciple of Pater, he became a practical, working writer, with a serviceable style.

Another point is suggested by Connolly's discussion. After listing a number of works in the modern movement (including *Sinister Street),* he asserts that one faith unites all the writers discussed (except G. B. Shaw and H. G. Wells): the sanctity of the artist. They are all inmates of the Ivory Tower, and the artist who accepts the religion of the Ivory Tower, of an art whose reward is perfection (which can only be attained by a separation of standards from those of the nonartist), may become a High Priest like James Joyce or W. B. Yeats, a Dandy like Ronald Firbank, an Incorruptible Observer like de Maupassant or Maugham, or a Detached Observer like Anatole France, but he will not be a Fighter or a Helper.[25] Mackenzie tells us that, when he went up to Oxford in 1901, he was buying *Yellow Books* and *Savoys* and "binding up a complete edition of Verlaine in a special shade of green buckram that took a week to meditate over. . . . "But he was also reading Montaigne, Rabelais, and Cervantes in ordinary serviceable editions.[26] He points out that the intense estheticism he displayed by the time he was fifteen was offset by militant Anglo-Catholicism: "I spent two years as a belligerent in the various brawls that took place in churches. . . . The lilies and languors of decadent literature were accompanied by the roses and raptures of hitting the noses of militant young Kensitites."[27] So it was wrong of Connolly to put him into the Ivory Tower; as we shall see, he was strongly influenced by one of Connolly's exceptions — H. G. Wells — and Wells was a Fighter.

III   Carnival

When Mackenzie's first novel was published, he felt that it was imperative for him to follow it up with a second as soon as possible. In the Octaves and elsewhere, he has given a great deal of information about the writing of that second novel, *Carnival.* The intimate knowledge of the *demi-monde* which it displays had come to him from personal experience:

> I had made friends . . . with a girl called Daisy, whose rent and household expenses . . . were paid by a commercial traveller and who was free when he was away to frequent the Café de l'Europe and the Café de Provence in Leicester Square without having to earn her living professionally. Daisy was the true *fille de joie* whose world was the underworld. . . . Thanks to her, my knowledge of London's underworld became as extensive and peculiar as Sam Weller's knowledge of London. . . . My friendship with Daisy was not a love-affair, but we shared a sense of humour and she was the perfect guide. Her gift as a *raconteuse* would only be surpassed when I met the original Jenny Pearl of *Carnival* five years later.[28]

The immediate impulse to write a novel dealing with the theater came from his experiences while working on a revue, *All Change Here,* during the closing months of 1910. It was produced by an ebullient and erratic theatrical impresario, H. G. Pélissier, then at the height of his fame as producer of the "Follies" at the Apollo Theatre; Mackenzie gives a vivid picture of him in Octave Four, and Faith confirms Mackenzie's account of the mad life they lived while under the dominance of Pélissier's whims in *As Much as I Dare*. For *All Change Here,* Mackenzie wrote the lyrics, selected the chorus girls, and helped with rehearsals. One of the girls of the ballet, Christine Maude, was the inspiration for his Jenny Pearl: "Miss Maude was twenty-four in that October; when these words are published she will be seventy-eight, the wife of my lifelong friend John Mavrogordato, to whom I dedicated the second volume of *Sinister Street.*"[29]

Having a character and setting in mind, Mackenzie was fortunate enough to hit on a plot. A man he saw lurking near the stage door one afternoon reminded him of a Cornish farmer he had known who had married a barmaid during a brief visit to London; the memory of "that lost peroxided London nymph" whom he had met in Cornwall and "the teetotal satyr who had carried her away" suggested a strange destiny for his heroine: "Upon the personality of Christine Maude I would build a story that would make Jenny Pearl marry Zachary Trewhella, the Cornish farmer who would kill her in the last chapter."[30]

The Cornish section occupies less than a fifth of the novel, however; for most of the narrative concerns Jenny's early years and stage life. Daughter of an attractive but discontented mother and an ineffectual father, she shows a natural talent for dancing, which is encouraged by a retired clown named Mr. Vergoe who is a roomer in their house. Through his insistence Jenny goes to Mme. Aldavini's ballet school; eventually, she becomes a member of the chorus at Covent Garden and Drury Lane. Mackenzie is very convincing in dealing with the growth of an artist; he depicts Jenny's early love for an audience, her enchantment when she first visits a theater, and her need for discipline but her impatience with it. With diligence she might become a prima ballerina, but she is lazy, and besides she has no impetus to improve, no vision of excellence. On impulse, she throws up every possibility of advancement by joining the chorus line at the Orient Palace of Varieties.

Her rebelliousness in this instance is only one aspect of her quarrel with the world; another is shown by her view of men as creatures to be used. She has a pleasant enough time amusing herself with a series of eager young men, all of them treated with contempt, until she falls in love with a young dilettante named Maurice Avery. Largely because of her mother, she refuses to become his mistress; she and

Maurice reach an impasse; and, when he is called abroad by the death of a relative, he deliberately terminates their relationship. When Jenny recovers from the wounds of this love affair, she is casually seduced by a veteran roué; almost as a retribution, her mother dies very soon after, and she is left with the responsibility for an invalid sister. This train of circumstances brings her to the mismatch with the Cornishman, Trewhella, and to the tragic ending brought about by his insane jealousy.

Mackenzie's desire to treat the theater realistically rather than sentimentally is worth noticing. It has its romantic and magical aspects; but, as time passes, these recede in importance: it becomes just the mechanical routine Jenny goes through each day before her real life begins. A similar realism extends to all the other settings, except perhaps the Cornish scene. Like Arnold Bennett, Mackenzie uses the background to establish the dimensions of a person's life; through a parlour in Bursley or a house in Paris, Bennett can show the way of life of his Five Towns characters and their inability to escape it, and similarly Mackenzie's description of Jenny's room when she is seventeen or the dressing room of the Orient Palace of Varieties — a long, low room of whitewashed brick, always dark and always hot, in which enchantment cannot possibly survive — establishes the meagerness of her possibilities. In *The Old Wives' Tale,* Bennett has Sophia reflect, "Once I was young and proud . . . "; Jenny's mother Mrs. Raeburn feels her life slipping on and reflects (thinking of herself), "once she was young and pretty. . . . " Jenny's favorite expression, "Who cares?" reflects the insouciance of a thwarted Columbine; she is dissatisfied with the pattern of her life yet unable to transcend the limitations of her environment.

But Mackenzie's description of limited lives is closer to Wells than to Bennett, though Jenny is a real-life person rather than — as Wells would make her — a sociological phenomenon. The poverty of her background is insisted on: "There was nothing to counterbalance the terrors of childhood in Hagworth Street. Outside the hope of one day being able to do as she liked, Jenny had no ideals. Worse, she had no fairyland."[31] Beside Wells's description of Kipps's or Mr. Polly's education, we can set Mackenzie's of Jenny's:

Her education at the board school was mechanical: the mistresses were like mental coffee-grinders who having absorbed a certain number of hard facts roasted by somebody else, distributed them in a more easily assimilated form. . . . It is important to understand the stark emptiness of Jenny's mind now and for a long while afterwards. Life was a dragging, weary affair unless she was being amused. There had been no mental adventures since, flashing and glorious, the idea of dancing came furiously through the night as she lay awake thinking of the pantomime.[32]

Mr. Vergoe is amusingly described as an ancient Mischief, a primordial spoiler of good order and domestic peace, who saw an artist in the making and was not concerned about anything else. The implication is that artistic training will not remedy the deficiencies of Jenny's early education; art will not be the means to a rich and full life. But Mackenzie's analysis of the crippling effects of environment takes him in a direction in which Wells would never go: he stresses Jenny's spiritual poverty. After saying that Jenny had no ideals and no fairyland, he asks, "And where was the Sunday-school with its angels of watchfulness and fiery saints?" This question provides an opportunity for a Wellsian caricature of a teacher who sniffed her way through a Cockney version of the Sermon on the Mount; but later, Mackenzie returns to the same problem: "Here was a child worthy of a Naiad's maternity. . . . and when for the first time she was given the world to look at her finite vision and infinite aspirations were never set in relation to each other. She was given a telescope, and nobody had taken off the shutter. Her soul was a singing bird in a cage. Freedom was the only ideal. She might have been moved by Catholicism, but nobody gave it to her."[33] In the course of his long career, Wells was to give many different answers to the question of why lives were stupid and narrow; in this passage, Mackenzie gave the one explanation which Wells would never have given.

Carnival reflects the influence of Wells in other ways too. Feminism, the theme of Wells's *Ann Veronica,* is briefly important when Jenny joins the suffragette movement and takes part in a march on Westminster. Much more important, however, are the techniques of humor which Mackenzie borrows from Wells, who in turn had got them from Dickens. For example, Uncle Pumblechook in Dickens's *Great Expectations* perhaps suggested a character in Wells's *Kipps* named Uncle Penstemon — and the latter's ludicrous behavior at a funeral certainly gave Mackenzie the idea of introducing Uncle James Threadgale at Mrs. Raeburn's funeral in *Carnival,* even though he did not take the humorous possibilities of the situation as far as Wells did. Wells's obsession with class also comes into *Carnival,* though Mackenzie is not preaching about the necessity of getting rid of class distinctions but merely showing that they exist and have profound consequences. Because of their different backgrounds, Maurice and Jenny could never have been happy together; they are aware of the problem and even discuss it, but it is brought out most effectively through Jenny's conversation:

> "Is that your mother?" asked Madge, pointing to Mona Lisa.
> "Don't be silly, Madge Wilson," Jenny corrected. "It's a picture, and I *don't* think much of her," she continued. "What a terrible mouth. Her hands is nice, though-very nice. And what's all those rocks at the back — low tide at Clacton, I should think."[34]

The time Mackenzie had spent in preparing a dramatic version of *Kipps* had not been wasted, even though the play never reached the stage; it had taught him to observe the speech of various classes of Londoners; and he put this knowledge to excellent use in *Carnival.*[35]

In *Literature in My Time,* Mackenzie explained the method of exposition he employed in *Carnival* and also defined its limitation: "Once when discussing with me my own novel *Carnival,* which was an attempt at the Flaubertian method of never allowing the chief character off the page, James said he doubted whether the figure of a ballet girl was substantial enough to sustain so much centralization, and in that criticism he put his finger on the weak spot of Flaubert's method, not for Flaubert himself, who never strained it by extending it indefinitely, but for novelists of less skill."[36]

As we have seen, Mackenzie feels free to comment on the action himself, rather than limiting himself to what Jenny sees and feels; still, he keeps our attention entirely on her. But perhaps he felt from the first the necessity of providing some interest for the reader besides that of observing a life which becomes one of dull routine. Bennett was satisfied with romanticizing some of the ordinary things in life, so that Cyril Baines's first day in school inspired his parents with a vision of the exceedingly romantic novelty of existence; much more romantic in temperament, Mackenzie had to whisk his reader away to an environment which was unlikely for his heroine (even though he had encountered such a situation in real life). But Kenneth Young is right, I think, when he refers to "Mackenzie's astonishing insight into the character of a small child who grows into a young woman but never into a mature woman," and to the fact that the real tragedy lies in the gradual waste of a life, not its termination by gunshot.[37] The Flaubertian method works, even though Mackenzie departs from verisimilitude in order to give his novel a theatrical conclusion.

CHAPTER 3

Sinister Street

I *An Experiment with Point of View*

FOR *Sinister Street* (1913), his third novel, Mackenzie followed Wells and Bennett in employing autobiographical material; rather than imitating them, however, he was reacting against them: "I felt that it was time an attempt was made to present in detail the youth of somebody handicapped by a public school and university education instead of poverty or more humble circumstances."[1] The first volume takes Michael Fane through a West Kensington boyhood, including prep school and public school (St. James' in the novel is obviously St. Paul's); the second volume (1914) describes his years at Oxford and his adventures in the London underworld. But Mackenzie insisted that the novel was not thinly disguised autobiography: Michael Fane "is to me an objective reality: he is not myself in a looking-glass."[2]

Mackenzie gave his hero an unconventional background; only after a certain Lord Saxby has been killed in the South African War do Michael and his sister Stella realize that they are the offspring of a liaison between Saxby and their mother. Mrs. Fane is like one of Shelley's phantoms of beauty, shadowy and rarely seen; since she is usually traveling with Saxby, she does not have the normal controlling influence of a mother over her children, and they are abandoned to a succession of governesses. Still, when Mackenzie used the word "handicapped", he was not applying it to these circumstances but to his hero's education; the schoolmasters at St. James' are caricatures, and the dons at Oxford are not sufficiently worthy of notice to be characterized at all. Yet Oxford itself is all-important; and, in attempting to define its essence, Mackenzie wrote what Mortimer Proctor, in his study of the subject, calls "in almost every way the best of all university novels. . . ."[3]

A novel which had to be published in two volumes and ran to 1132 pages was bound to be called diffuse and formless; nevertheless Mackenzie was trying to use an even more disciplined technique than he had employed in *Carnival:* "In constructing *Sinister Street,* besides avoiding anything outside the ken of my chief figure, Michael Fane, I was more successful in avoiding psychologizing about his thoughts and behavior than I had been over Jenny Pearl, and also in keeping out any suggestion of comment, direct or implied by myself as author. I wanted Michael Fane's attitude to life to remain what it was at the time."[4] In the foreword to a new edition of *Sinister Street* (1949), he wrote that, in reading the novel through for the first time since he had written it, he was "relieved to find that the technique which aimed to keep the reader at the same age as the principal character has been effective."[5]

The use of this technique suggests some resemblance to Joyce's *Portrait of the Artist as a Young Man,* which began to appear in *The Egoist* in February, 1914, five months after the publication of the first volume of *Sinister Street.* The *Portrait* begins, "Once upon a time and a very good time it was there was a moocow coming down along the road. . . ." The first sentence of *Sinister Street* is, "From a world of daisies as big as moons and of mountainous green hillocks Michael Fane came, by some unrealized method of transport, to the thin red house that as yet for his mind could not claim an individual existence amid the uniformity of a long line of fellows." Obviously there *is* a difference; Michael's limited awareness is demonstrated through a language and a perspective that are not his. A few sentences farther on, Michael inspects the bars of his cot: "for Michael each bar possessed a personality. Minute scratches unnoticed by the heedless adult world lent variety of expression: slight irregularities infused certain groups with an air of deliberate consultation. From the four corners royal bars, crowned with brass, dominated their subjects. Passions, intrigues, rumours, ambitions, revenges were perceived by Michael to be guarded by a romantic population, with one or two of whose units Michael could willingly have dispensed: one bar in particular, set very much askew, seemed sly and malignant."[6]

Again, the language is not a child's language; and the passage is in part an invitation to the "heedless adult world" to recognize that a child's point of view is different from its own. As for the attribution of personality to iron bars — particularly the view that one of them is malignant — there is something grotesque here in the manner of

Dickens. A page and a half farther on, when Michael's sister Stella begins "to chant her saga" — "Primitive and immemorial sounds flowed from that dewy mouth; melodies and harmonies, akin to the day itself, voiced the progress of the clouds. . . ." — we are clearly listening as mature adults capable of perceiving something enchanting and immemorial in her humming.

Nevertheless Michael's perspective and his emotions are presented in a very authentic way. We learn to judge, as he does, in terms of what is to be feared and what is not; there are many itinerant terrors haunting the roads, the worst being chimney sweeps — Michael hides under the dining-room table until one passes. On the whole, we stay with the boy's consciousness and follow his development. By the time book 2, "Classic Education," has been reached, we are certainly looking at life with his eyes. In the second chapter, for example, Michael is shocked to hear that his sister is going to Germany to study music: "To Michael this step seemed a device to spoil Stella beyond the limits of toleration, and he thought with how many new affectations Stella would return to her native land. . . . Michael felt strongly that the balance of life was heavily weighted in favour of girls and he deplored the blindness of grown-up people unable to realize the greater attractiveness of boys. It was useless for Michael to protest, although he wasted an evening of Henty in arguing the point with Miss Carthew."[7] In book 3, "Dreaming Spires," we are with Michael from his first day, first week, and first term at university until his last term, last week, and last day — and we absorb its atmosphere as he does:

Michael sitting snugly in the morning quiet of his room, leaned over to poke the fire into a blaze, eyed with satisfaction November's sodden mists against his window and settled himself back in the deep chair. . . .

It was so restful to stare up at Mona Lisa and traverse without fatigue that labyrinth of rocks and streams. His desk not yet deranged by work or correspondence possessed a monumental stability of neatness that was most soothing to contemplate. It had the restfulness of a well-composed landscape where every contour took the eye easily onward and where every tree grew just where it was needed for a moment's halt. The olive-green magazine dropped unregarded on the floor, and there was no other book within reach. The dancing fire danced on. Far away sounded the cries of daily life. The chimes in St. Mary's tower struck without proclaiming any suggestion of time. How long these roll-call mornings were and how rapidly dream on dream piled its drowsy outline. Was there not somewhere at the other end of Oxford a lecture at eleven o'clock? This raw morning was not suitable for lectures out of college. Was not Maurice coming to lunch? How deliciously far off was the time for ordering lunch. He really must get out of the habit of sitting in this deep wicker-chair. . . .[8]

By the method James Joyce adopted in the *Portrait,* Marvin Magalaner and R. M. Kain write, he accomplished two things: he eliminated the omniscient narrator and therefore the explicit moralizing on man and nature which Samuel Butler found indispensable in *The Way of All Flesh,* and he brought the reader into the picture as an active participant in the experience.[9] Mackenzie had a similar desire to eliminate whatever would hinder the reader from feeling just what it was like to be at Oxford during Michael Fane's period there. Arnold Bennett found fault with the action of the novel: "The invention is very poor: this is not a matter of argument, as its conventionality and facility can be demonstrated."[10] Although this criticism applies justly to the last part of the novel, in which Michael Fane follows Butler's Ernest Pontifex into the meaner quarters of London, it shows little awareness of what Mackenzie was trying to do in the Oxford chapters. When thanking Ronald Knox for the second volume of *Sinister Street,* Guy Lawrence wrote, "The Oxford part is singularly good to my mind. The absence of incident is especially good and clever."[11] The same emphasis on mood or texture of experience is to be found in Max Beerbohm's praise of *Sinister Street* as the best book on Oxford ever written: "There is no book on Oxford like it. It gives you actual Oxford *experience.* What Mackenzie has miraculously done is to make you feel what each *term* was like. . . ."[12] This effect was not accomplished by accident, and Mackenzie undoubtedly had a right to complain that the careful handling of point of view in the novel had not received critical attention: "What no critic has noted is that the scheme of the book demands from the reader that he should identify himself with the principal character through whose eyes he is compelled to look at life."[13]

II *The Development of a Personality*

In a survey of the reviews, Erlandson finds that two main criticisms were made of *Sinister Street:* that its central character was only a person to whom things happened, the passive recipient of impressions, and that it was lacking in plot.[14] These two criticisms were linked with a third in Edmund Wilson's discussion of Mackenzie's influence on the early F. Scott Fitzgerald; concerning the American's *This Side of Paradise,* he wrote:

> It has almost every fault and deficiency that a novel can possibly have. It is not only highly imitative but it imitates an inferior mode. Fitzgerald, when he wrote the book, was drunk with Compton Mackenzie, and it sounds like an American attempt to rewrite *Sinister Street.* Now Mackenzie, in spite of his gift for picturesque and comic invention and the capacity for pretty writing that he says he learned from Keats, lacks both the intellectual force and the emotional language to give body and outline to the material which he secretes in such enormous abundance. With the seeds he took from Keats's garden, one of the best-arranged gardens in England, he exfloreated so profusely that he blotted out the path of his own. Michael Fane, the hero of *Sinister Street,* was swamped in the forest of description; he was smothered by creepers and columbine. From the time he went up to Oxford, his personality began to grow dimmer. . . .[15]

In reply to this very severe criticism, we need to analyze what happens to Michael in some detail. First of all, he *is* an observer rather than a doer in the novel; Erlandson writes that "Michael's environment, both mental and physical, and his experiences are essentially those of Mackenzie himself,"[16] but at Oxford he does not write, act, or debate, much less carry on a dozen such activities simultaneously as did Isis Idol No. 259. Fane is temperamentally different from Mackenzie, and he also develops more slowly. As a novel dealing with the formation of a personality, *Sinister Street* shows various influences shaping an impressionable young man; and, as Mackenzie says in the epilogue, he is still growing.

Though we usually adopt his point of view in the novel, there are places where we stand aside from him and smile at his immature behavior. Many times, for example, he plays the censorious older brother to his sister: "He felt almost a responsibility with regard to Stella, a highly moral sensation of knowing better the world and its pitfalls than she could."[17] He is also dealt with ironically in a romantic escapade with a certain Kathleen — after she has left for good, he enters her hotel room and salvages the only souvenir he can find, a cake of soap. His phase of extreme piety is equally amusing; he fills his room with "eikons, scapulars, crucifixes, candlesticks" and has a map on the wall identifying all the High Anglican churches in the United Kingdom. Wilson is on good ground when he satirizes the flowers from Keats's garden; in fact, Erlandson gives a long list of oddities of diction in the last part of the novel. But Erlandson also writes, "Mackenzie seeks to adapt his expression to the age and general awareness of his central character."[18] The style mirrors Michael's consciousness at a particular time; the Keatsian vocabulary, with certain exceptions, fits where it is used — especially in the Oxford section, where it helps convey the texture of Michael's experience.

As to the other main criticism of the novel, even the *Daily Mail* review which sent the novel on its way to popular success admitted its validity; Mackenzie "set to work on *Sinister Street* with no particular scheme or plot in his head. He just wrote and wrote of everything that he had experienced from the age of three or thereabouts."[19] But the novel has a clear and functional plot; it is the story of a quest for a pattern of conduct. Michael possesses a status in society despite his illegitimacy, but he has no father to guide him or to provide him with a pattern of behavior either to imitate or to react against. The strongest influence on his early life is his governess Miss Carthew, who appears like a fairy princess to him. In a literal sense, his life has been dismal before her arrival: "Nurse's crabbed face and stunted figure had hitherto . . . dominated . . . his solitary childhood. Michael had for so long been familiar with ugliness that he was dangerously near to an eternal imprisonment in a maze of black fancies."[20] Miss Carthew brings him a new apprehension of beauty, and appropriately takes him to an enchanted palace, her home in Hampshire, with a garden which he considers the most beautiful in the world. The romantic and idealistic approach to existence which she encourages remains with him; later, he envisages the girl of his dreams as ineffable and impalpable: "Somewhere beneath that sable diadem of chimney tops she lay, that lovely girl of his desire. He would not picture her too clearly lest he should destroy the charm of his amazing impotence of longing."[21]

As time goes on, Michael finds that (like Stephen Dedalus) he has to fly past nets set to catch him: his mother's desire that he will be an agreeable companion for her when she happens to want one; his school's, that he conform to expectations and win a scholarship to Oxford; his schoolmates', that he conform to the group; the esthete Wilmot's, that he become a decadent; and a host of others. At times, he seems to have a Byronic thirst for new sensations and to refuse any commitment whatsoever: he "vowed that he would go heedless of everything that stood between him and experience. He would deny himself nothing: he would prove to the hilt everything."[22] Ultimately, however, he responds to Miss Carthew's appeal that he be a Christian gentleman.

His quest involves redefining the concept of a gentleman in terms appropriate to his times. The quixotic aspect of his character is emphasized throughout; in his yearly rereading of Cervantes's classic, he finds in it "more and more certainly all that was most vital to life's appreciation." He regrets the passing of a chivalric ethos: "Something akin to Don Quixote's impulsive dismay Michael experienced in his own view of the twentieth century. He felt the need of a constructive ideal of conduct to sustain him through the long pilgrimage that must ensue after these hushed Oxford dreams."[23] Feeling himself a member of a special class, he is always aware not of his privileges but of his responsibilities; after Stella and he have encountered a wild boar in the forest of Compiègne, for example, he "wished that all his life he might stand between her and the world, the blundering wild-boar of a world."[24] When he dines with Prescott, an old friend of his father's, at a 'modish cloister," the Albany, he feels the attraction of a life of bachelor ease — but Prescott's suicide soon after throws him back forcibly on his earlier view that a life of withdrawal will not do. Similarly, he samples but rejects the religion of Good Eggery: "Oxford was divided into Bad Men and Good Eggs. The Bad Men went up to London and Womanized — some even of the worst womanized in Oxford: they dressed in a style that either by its dowdiness or its smartness stamped them. . . . The Good Eggs went up to London and got drunk; and if they womanized no one must know anything about it. . . ."[25] The "four plastic years" Michael spends at Oxford are years in which he analyzes both his own capacities and various models of behavior. They do not make him subscribe to Good Eggery or any other pattern of conformity; instead, they result in his following his own concept of a gentleman, whose paradoxical way of serving society is by opposing it. This opposition implies a judgment on his world. Early in the book, contemporary standards are occasionally called into question, as when Mrs. Frith the cook gets drunk and is summarily ordered off the premises; and a policeman is called to escort her on her way. Later, Michael reacts strongly against certain aspects of Victorianism — in particular to the excesses of patriotic frenzy over the Boer War. Yet he remains in his society instead of opting out of it, as Joyce's Stephen Dedalus and as Butler's Ernest Pontifex do. He does so partly because, though he has little rapport with any of his teachers, there is a succession of older people — especially Miss Carthew, her mother, and Father Viner — from whom he can receive sympathetic understanding. However, he has to make a commitment; and he makes it after following the heroes of George Gissing and Butler (and preceding Maugham's) into the mean streets of London to arrive at a resolution which none of these others makes: the necessity for moral choice. He feels a quixotic responsibility for a girl he has known who is leading a dissolute life; only a lucky chance saves him from marrying her. Finally, he makes the equally quixotic decision of defending against society a worthless murderer, Harry Meats. "You want to strike at the foundations of the legal system," says a barrister; and Michael replies, "Exactly." He has taken up this cause because he views society as a heartless mechanism, "a great complication of machinery fed by gold and directed by fear," which is willing enough to execute the criminal but does nothing to remove the injustice which causes crime. Setting himself against the values of the hive or the ant-hill, Michael is on the way to adopting an unusual vocation: he seems likely to become a priest.

III   *Secondary Characters*

I have stressed the main line of action affecting the central character of *Sinister Street* because its importance is easily missed. What is most obvious in the novel is Mackenzie's successful creation of a whole host of secondary characters. Michael's Oxford friends are marvelously individuated, and Mackenzie is very skillful in showing the subtle effects which the university has on them — as on Michael's best friend Alan Merivale, who becomes for a time a fussy old Christ Church bachelor who complains that every one else in his college is dull. Many of the more vivid characters are amusingly treated; after the death of Lord Saxby, Michael's mother turns from one fad to another — Mental Science, an association to prevent premature burial, a Society for Agricultural Labourers, a society for the abatement of London street noises — and she becomes an amiable eccentric. Several of the humorous characters are taken from real life; the cook was a real cook in the Compton household, and Mrs. Frith was her actual name, as Mackenzie explains: "I called her Mrs. Frith in *Sinister Street* because I could not find a name that did not somehow detract from the invaluable service she performed for me by letting fresh air into that house and lightening the oppression of my old nurse's rule."[26] Of these characters the most important and most fully developed is Venner, steward of the Junior Common Room at St. Mary's and tutelary spirit of the College; this is an affectionate portrait of Richard Gunstone, or "Gunner," who was so much a part of Magdalen College as Mackenzie remembered it.

The novel was a considerable success as the portrait of an age. Ford Madox Ford wrote, *"Sinister Street* is really history — the history of a whole class, in a whole region, during a whole period of life." C. K. Shorter wrote, "the real job of Mr. Mackenzie's book to me is that it is the best modern novel of London life — the London that I know."[27] Paradoxically, as Erlandson shows, the very fact that it evoked a world so well counted against it during the 1920's: it suffered *because* it gave an excellent picture of an era which the 1920's wanted to despise or to forget.[28] Its influence was enormous (as on the early F. Scott Fitzgerald), but it was comparatively short-lived; it suffered an eclipse from which it has never recovered. The Oxford section is a masterpiece; the concluding section is perhaps disappointing, yet the novel as a whole deserves much more careful reading than it has usually received.

CHAPTER 4

The Theatre of Youth

I N Mackenzie's chapter on "The Years Before the War" in *Literature in My Time,* he writes that he had "designed *Sinister Street* to be one of two preludes to a complete survey of contemporary society in which the personages of a large and complicated series of books were to be shown in youth."[1] He associates this ambitious plan with the desire of many writers of the era to extend the scope of the novel, either in reaction against the deliberately contrived and artificial novel or in response to the influence of the Russians. The new movement spread right across Europe: "Romain Rolland in France had just produced the eight or nine volumes of *Jean Christophe,* and Marcel Proust in 1911 had just published the first volume of that huge work *À la Recherche du Temps Perdu.* I remember Edmund Gosse's telling me he had just read a French novel that seemed to him an example of the same kind of impulse which had led me into writing *Sinister Street.* . . ."[2] In England, Mackenzie continues, Arnold Bennett, J. D. Beresford, and others were beginning to write trilogies; and Galsworthy, though without the initial intention of doing so, was to protract his account of the Forsytes into a saga.

As Michael Sadleir pointed out in 1929, the vogue for long novels perhaps represented a return to the Victorian three-decker; and Erlandson has found a statement in which Mackenzie in effect says this in 1913.[3] Yet, as J. W. Beach writes, something else must have inspired "that predilection for novels in series which has been a leading feature of the early twentieth century."[4] In Mackenzie's case, the model for a sequence of novels was Balzac, whom he had begun reading with fascination at the age of seventeen: "Oh, to read *Eugènie Grandet* now and be able to find myself sitting paralysed with the emotion of it and unable to turn over the next page in the dread of hearing old Grandet ask his daughter for the coins in the money-box which she had given to her lover!"[5] He also writes that in 1918 "I was still supposing that I should carry on my Comédie Humaine [Balzac's term] to be called The Theatre of Youth."[6] He wanted to give a detailed picture of his generation, as Balzac had done, by following the French writer's method of writing a series of separate but interconnected novels. "My original plan," Mackenzie wrote, "was to take the subsidiary characters of *Sinister Street,* one after another, and make them principals in other books."[7]

As for what happened to his plan, "I stuck to this idea, as in *Guy and Pauline, Sylvia Scarlett,* and *The Vanity Girl,* until I was compelled to recognize that the First World War had smashed the series of linked novels I intended to call *The Theatre of Youth,* because I should never be able to escape from it." He means that he would have had to make the war the climactic event in the life of each of his young people in turn, and "The First World War as a *deus ex machina* would soon have become intolerable to myself and to my readers." In the foreword from which these comments about "The Theatre of Youth" come, he quotes Lascelles Abercrombie's impression of *Sinister Street:* "We seem to be watching that strangest of all modes of evolution, the dissolution of one century's character to make way for the character of another century."[8] If his real interest in "The Theatre of Youth" novels was not in describing the effect of the war, it was probably in picturing as accurately as possible what it meant to be a member of the generation which was coming to maturity just as the twentieth century began.

I Guy and Pauline

Guy and Pauline (1915) has close links with his two previous novels. Guy Hazlewood is a contemporary of Michael Fane at Oxford; and his house Plashers Mead, in the Cotswold village of Wychford, is one which he and Michael found on a cycling trip described in *Sinister Street.* Michael appears frequently in *Guy and Pauline,* and the novel ends with the two friends in Italy where Michael is going into a Benedictine monastery. In this concluding episode, Guy reads Michael a letter from Maurice Avery in which he says that he has just seen the Orient ballet and fallen in love with a girl named Jenny Pearl. The novels in "The Theatre of Youth" cycle are very different from each other, but characters and even episodes in one novel often have an important bearing on one another.

Mackenzie began writing *Guy and Pauline* on Capri on New Year's Eve, 1914. On April 4, when he had written 270 pages and still had 125 to go, he received a letter from an old friend, Orlo Williams, telling him that General Sir Ian Hamilton had a place on his staff for him: after months of trying, he was suddenly going on active service. As if this news did not give him enough distraction from his writing, he suffered an attack of neuritis which almost paralyzed him; but he finished the novel in bed on the last day of April. A few days later he left for the Dardanelles — so that, ironically, his romantic idyll set in the pastoral Cotswolds is dedicated to a general and his staff and its proofs were corrected within range of Turkish guns.

When the friends first discover Wychford, Michael tells Guy that it is a place of dreams in which everything will turn into a radiant unreality and time will mean no more than a brief disturbance of sound. Lured from his room by a great moon the color of dislustered gold, Guy walks through an orchard in which the heavy mist makes the tree tops seem floating away from invisible trunks, and exclaims, "By gad, if I can't write here, I ought to be shot." Soon he meets the three daughters of the Reverend Mr. Grey, Rector of Wychford — Monica, Margaret, and Pauline, the last a "briar rose . . . whose petals seemed to fall at the touch of definition. . . . " With Pauline, of course, he falls in love; and a great deal of the book consists simply of passionate declarations in appropriate settings, such as the meadows by the Greenrush River or the hills around Wychford where flowers appropriate to the season bloom: in Michael Arlen's *The Green Hat,* Mackenzie's novel is referred to as "a garden catalogue."[9] A critic in *The Outlook* wrote, "Perhaps this is the most sentimental book that was ever written."[10]

But the discovery of Guy and Pauline that they love each other is made in the first quarter of the book; the reader who thinks that the rest of the book consists of romantic effusions has somehow ignored the difficulties which Mackenzie has put in the way of his lovers. He is telling, with variations, his own story — of his withdrawal from Oxford to Burford to write poetry, of his refusal to follow the career expected of him (in the novel, schoolteaching instead of acting), and of his own engagement at the age of twenty-one. That engagement ended unhappily; so does this one. "Mr. Compton Mackenzie has made himself a cobweb glittering with dewdrops," wrote one disappointed reviewer, "and then put his foot through it."[11] Idyllic as the novel may appear, therefore, it is chiefly the story of the disintegration of a love which seemed perfect and enduring. Three lines from

Robert Browning's "The Statue and the Bust," which Guy says haunts him, describe what takes place:

> So weeks grew months, years; gleam by gleam
> The glory dropped from their youth and love,
> And both perceived they had dreamed a dream; . . .

The action of the novel, therefore, does not consist principally of external events but of the subtle changes in the two principal characters and in their relationship. Mackenzie's own memories enable him to describe the stages in minute detail, not only from Guy's point of view but from Pauline's. But occasionally he calls in the aid of literary precedent; as Erlandson shows, he sees the need of an objective correlative for the private world of feeling; and, like many a writer before him (his favorite novelist Hardy among them), he finds it in nature. If rainy weather or a field of daffodils says something about a character's mood and feelings, the progress of the seasons also serves a special purpose: "the pageant of the year's seasons becomes the external index of the progress of the affair, which likewise proves cyclic."[12]

Sometimes Mackenzie uses his borrowed devices in a melodramatic way; this is especially true of the half-ruined Wychford Abbey and the mill pond near it, places which for Pauline are full of terror and ill omen — as they might obviously have been for Hardy. (It is noteworthy that Pauline, like Tess Durbeyfield, is referred to as a wounded bird.) But, on the whole, in his description of the state of tension under which his two people live during their long engagement, Mackenzie seems close to the mind's actual way of working. The story tells how a friendly and helpful family begins to seem like spies to the two lovers; of how Pauline in fantasy sees Guy spinning away from her into the void; of how Guy becomes brutal towards Pauline simply because of his own uncertainty about the future — then, conscious that he abuses her love, he wonders in dismay if his love is not being destroyed by some fatal impulse at the back of his own mind.

When Guy eventually publishes a book of poetry, he has so little regard for it that he decides to have it appear anonymously. Pauline ruefully sees his reaction as a condemnation of her; can she think of herself as essential to him, if this is the best he can do under her influence? Will he not one day listen to the words of his Oxford friends, who tell him that he is stagnating in the country? But, if there are difficulties over money and the choice of a career, a special area of conflict is religion. It is of central importance to the Grey family; Monica, in fact, decides to become an Anglican nun. Guy goes to church to please Pauline, but she makes it clear that he does so for the worst of reasons: a kind of fair-weather spoiling of her. The handling of the question is interesting because Guy begins to see religion not merely as a decorative adjunct to Pauline but as something in her very being — and therefore very menacing to him: "Pauline actually believed in her religion, believed in it to the extent of dishonouring their love to appease the mumbo-jumbo. That something so monstrously inexistent could have any such power was barely comprehensible, and yet here he was faced with what easily might prove to be a force powerful enough to annihilate their love."[13] He realizes that he has been playing with damnable insincerities: "to compare himself with the lover of The Blessed Damozel had been a luxurious melancholy. Pauline and he had worshipped together in chapels of Lyonesse where, if he had knelt beside her with rather a tender condescension toward her prayers, he had always been moved sincerely by the decorative appeal they made to him."[14] Even if he cannot accept Pauline's religion, it makes him a less superficial person than he has been.

Pauline does not change basically. Illustrating the axiom that love can occupy most of woman's existence but only part of man's, Guy begins to visit London, acquire new interests, and develop a life which she does not share. The breaking point is reached on the day when Margaret marries her Richard, one of the good solid Richards of England, as Guy terms him. Guy tells Pauline that his poems have outlived their date, and she asks, "Guy, could I outlive my date?" After conventional protestations to the contrary, he admits that he might temporarily become interested in another girl, though Pauline would always be first in his thoughts.

> "But you might be interested?" Pauline asked breathlessly.
> "I must be free if I'm going to be an artist."
> "Free?" she echoed slowly.

That evening she writes a note to him that breaks their engagement. The novel ends with each of them puzzling over where they diverged and struck by the fact of loss: "Her father of course would never speak of that broken engagement, and already she had made her mother promise never to speak of it again. Deep to her inmost heart only these familiar vales and streams and green meadows would speak of it for the rest of her life." As for Guy, he tells Michael, " . . . all my life I'll do penance for having said that an artist must be free."

Mackenzie is able to give a certain depth to Guy and Pauline and also Monica and Margaret. Erlandson finds the minor characters unsatisfactory, however, because they are "tagged."[15] Mrs. Peasey, Guy's housekeeper, is deaf as an adder, so that every conversation between them proceeds at cross-purposes. "Rather unfurnished, I'm afraid," Guy says, and she answers, "Oh, yes, I'm quite used to the country." Pauline's spinster friend Miss Verney is the daughter of a sailor and has had an unhappy love affair when she was young; these two facts about her are mentioned every time she appears. The Rector is passionately fond of gardening and always has a trowel in his hand and the Latin names for flowers on his lips. His wife has an air of vagueness and ineffectuality and is devoted to music. It is easy to see, then, that Mackenzie creates caricatures or types; yet he tries to give them some complexity, as by showing that Mrs. Grey is more capable of dealing with practical affairs than is immediately apparent and by giving the Rector an ironic manner which suggests that he knows something about other matters besides horticulture.

Mackenzie writes that, after the criticism of formlessness in *Sinister Street,* "I was determined to show with *Guy and Pauline* that I could tackle as difficult a piece of construction as any novelist could set himself, by composing a sort of violin and piano sonata."[16] The book covers a two-year span, and it is divided into chapters named after the seasons — chapter 1 is "Autumn" and chapter 5 "Another Autumn." Each chapter is in turn subdivided into three sections named after the months with which it deals. This arrangement may look very artificial, but it has a special meaning: time is of the utmost importance in the theme of the dying of love. When Mackenzie mentions a violin and piano sonata, he is alluding to another device: he tells the story in the third person but alternates between points of view, so that the "September" section of chapter 1 is basically Guy's story and the "October" Pauline's. What he is emphasizing through this contrivance is that the story is not, as might be expected, a passage from the life of Guy Hazlewood but the account of the relationship between the two central characters. The disciplined technique is perhaps responsible for the high reputation which the novel has had at certain times. In *The Georgian Literary*

Scene, Frank Swinnerton wrote that it was upon *Sinister Street* and *Guy and Pauline* that Mackenzie's fame rested and that *Guy and Pauline* was always considered to be his best novel by those who were not troubled with its sentiment.[17]

II *Sylvia Scarlett: The Picaresque Saint*

From an unwritten novel of Robert Louis Stevenson's with the projected title of *Sophia Scarlett,* Mackenzie got the surname for a subordinate character in *Sinister Street,* Sylvia Scarlett. She became the heroine of a novel he began in November, 1917, while he was on Capri on sick leave — on sick leave, and planning to write a 300,000-word novel in three months! Because of the wartime paper shortage, he relates, he had to write the first part of the novel on the manuscript of *Guy and Pauline* turned upside down. The war also caused the novel to appear in two parts, the first under the title *The Early Life and Adventures of Sylvia Scarlett* in August, 1918; the second, as *Sylvia and Michael* in March, 1919.

Kenneth Young quotes Mackenzie's statement that this was the first novel to be "affected by weariness and the disgust of war," and then he indicates his disagreement: "This does not strike the reader today. It is a book tingling with robust life and inexhaustible invention, not least in the latter pages of its heroine's traverse of war-time Europe."[18] Frieda Lawrence praised it enthusiastically: "You have not only given me two books, but a whole world, just a world that I am walking into, I am just in Spain with the nice fat old woman and Sylvia. That's picaresque, isn't it? . . . I love this book — Lawrence's new book has something of the quality of yours; I think that same having left all Englishness! — with I suppose the best of England in it. . . . "[19] Lawrence himself was also congratulatory: " . . . I've read *Sylvia Scarlett* and S. and Michael — amusing and witty and alas, only too like life." He adds, "This rolling stone business gets a little heartrending in the end. One is rather busy at it oneself. Poor Sylvia — qu'est-il donc qu'elle cherche? It isn't merely adventure. She's all the while looking for something *permanent.* Don't like the Christ hankering — sign of defeat: alas, S. and Michael are wistful pair."[20] Alas, there were more things to worry about in the novel than Sylvia's longing for religious certainty.

Before one of her early adventures, Sylvia sits down with a novel: "It was still impossibly early for an escape, so Sylvia sat down on the edge of her bed and composed herself to read the escape of Fabrizio from the Sforza tower in Parma."[21] Mackenzie thus confesses his own interest in Stendhal. In his memoirs, he relates that, when he was so ill with dysentery that he thought he was going to die, and told this to his friend Hope-Johnstone. Hope-Johnstone objected, "But you haven't read *War and Peace* yet." He lived to read both *War and Peace* and the other book Hope-Johnstone forced on him, the *Chartreuse de Parme;* both made the strongest impression on him: "*War and Peace* may have given me back the will to live, out of the life Tolstoy poured into that great book, but the *Chartreuse de Parme* gave me the assurance that life was worth writing about as well as living."[22]

Of Stendhal's two masterpieces, Mackenzie was immediately influenced by the one which contained a less disciplined structure. In Balzac's famous exposition of the plot of the *Chartreuse,* he describes just one part as like a canvas fifty feet by thirty. So Mackenzie began his novels with Stendhal's vast canvas in mind; Balzac takes forty pages for his plot summary,[23] and *Sylvia Scarlett* would take almost as many. With Sylvia, we begin in France and travel to a dozen other countries in Europe as well as North and South America; one wild unmotivated adventure succeeds another; and the tribute of imitation is paid to such legendary types of national violence as the flash of knives in Spain and the light-hearted display of shooting accuracy in Argentina. The robust life to which Young calls attention is certainly there; so is Lawrence's quest motif; so is an excellent depiction of refugee life in war-torn Europe. Still, the prodigal invention of characters and incidents ceases at times to have much significance, so that, whereas Balzac can find a unity in the composition of the *Chartreuse,* Mackenzie's *Sylvia Scarlett* seems not so much plotted as strung together.

The novel has often been called picaresque; Robertson writes, for example, "*Sylvia Scarlett* must unhesitatingly be classed as a picaresque novel; and it is one of the best specimens that have appeared in modern times."[24] In his excellent book *Literature and the Delinquent,* Alexander A. Parker complains that the term *picaresque* has been so misused that it has lost its usefulness: it seems only a synonym for *episodic.* To illustrate what he means, he quotes a passage from Robert Alter's *Rogue's Progress:* "the picaroon may have natural inclinations towards roguery, but he is not by nature a scoundrel . . . he demonstrates some strength in the virtues of the heart. . . . For perhaps the most basic assumption underlying the picaresque world view is the conviction that while life is hard, life is also good. . . . Without this supposition that man is basically decent, or at least that some men are decent, the picaresque virtues of compassion and companionship would be totally inexplicable." "Anyone familiar with Spanish literature," comments Parker, "can only gasp at the phrase 'the picaresque virtues of compassion and companionship.' Alter can write it without turning a hair, because by jumping the 161 years between *Lazarillo de Tormes* and *Gil Blas* he excludes from his account of the picaroon all the Spanish examples. . . ."[25] He himself prefers *delinquent* to *rogue* as the term which best conveys to our minds the sense of one who is an offender against the moral and civil laws — not a vicious criminal but someone who is dishonorable and antisocial in a much less violent way. Undoubtedly, Parker would feel that R. W. B. Lewis's title *The Picaresque Saint* is a contradiction; yet perhaps it gives a fairly accurate description of Sylvia Scarlett.[26]

Parker considers that the distinguishing feature of the *genre* is the atmosphere of delinquency. "This begins," he writes, "in a setting of low life but generally ascends the social scale; the origins of the protagonist are usually disreputable; he is either born or plunged as a youth into an environment of cheating and thieving, and learns to make his way in the world by cheating and thieving in his turn."[27] Born in Lille of a French mother and an English father, Sylvia is only eleven when her mother dies and her ne'er-do-well father (whose name is Henry Snow) takes her to England with him; and she is thus introduced into a world of seedy boardinghouses, traveling entertainers, blackmailers, and petty confidence men. This atmosphere sharpens her wits: she always seems old beyond her years. When she is sixteen, her father's girl friend deserts him and he commits suicide; she is left with no one in the world except her father's unsavory partner, Jimmy Monkley. It is not long before he locks her bedroom door and tries to make love to her; she escapes from the boardinghouse, and from this time on she is entirely on her own — so that the interest resides in watching a young girl live by her wits and still retain her respectability. In a world of thievery and cheating, she manages to survive without becoming a thief and a cheat herself; she remains essentially untouched by her environment.

For a near delinquent, she is remarkably intellectual. At seventeen, for example, she is reading Petronius and deciding that his interpretation of the world squares with her own. So when she meets a Balliol graduate, Philip Iredale, he finds her refreshing and fascinating; and he is soon asking her to marry him. The marriage takes place, but Sylvia soon finds that her husband is less advanced and unconventional in his views than he had seemed to be. He is another Angel Clare, shown as a snobbish hater of clergymen and "low" people; and he relapses into stony respectability when some malicious scandal is spread about Sylvia and an eccentric minister named Mr. Dorward. When Philip becomes Victorian and forbids her to see Dorward, she leaves him — and lives three months as a prostitute to pay him back for her clothing and for anything else she has received from him.

Now her life of wandering begins as an actress and cabaret singer; also during this time she takes charge of Lily Haden and tries to prevent her from marrying Michael Fane. Out of her many adventures, she is eventually able to put together a series of stage improvisations which secures her something of a triumph in London; thus she is able to impose an imaginative unity on her life, which comes chiefly through a sensitive understanding and portrayal of people who have intrigued her. Before this success, she has had a wildly improbable meeting with Arthur Madden, whom she had known in London when she was sixteen, in Sulphurville, Indiana. After nursing him through an illness, she becomes his mistress — which seems incredible, since he is shown as spineless, weak, and whining. Finally resolving that she cannot live on her own, she decides to marry him; when everything is ready for the wedding however, he elopes with someone else. The end of the *Early Adventures* shows her shattered by this experience and determined to leave England in spite of her triumph in the theater.

As the title of the continuation suggests, Michael comes into her life again. This occurs only after she has had typhus fever in Russia, recovered to find the world at war, and drifted southward closer and closer to a zone of hostilities. On the way, she has taken a Spanish dancer named Concetta under her wing; Concetta now calls herself Queenie Walters and wants to be thought of as English. As earlier Sylvia found a sense of purpose in keeping Lily Haden on the straight and narrow, so now she tries to keep Queenie out of the clutches of a brutal German juggler whose stage name is Zozo. Poverty and precarious circumstances help Zozo to win and Sylvia, again on her own, finds herself traveling from Bulgaria into Serbia shortly before the Bulgarian declaration of war. At Nish she is detained for questioning, and receives the help of a British officer stationed there, Guy Hazlewood; he tells her that Michael is also in Serbia.

She is in Nish when it is overrun by Bulgarian troops; by this time,

Guy has been wounded fighting for the Serbians, and he dies after giving her a letter for Michael to take to Miss Pauline Grey, Wychford Rectory, Oxfordshire. Michael himself arrives at Nish, apparently dying of typhus, and in the care of his sister Stella. Sylvia persuades Stella to leave while she can and to let her nurse Michael instead, Sylvia and Michael are interned by the Bulgarians, and eventually a Bulgarian leader requites a favor done him by Sylvia by helping the two of them escape into neutral Greece. For Michael this has been the most perfect companionship possible for human beings, and in the last pages of the novel he asks her to marry him.

As this summary indicates, the plot requires more coincidences than should be allowed in a dozen novels. Even those already mentioned do not exhaust the list, for Sylvia's former husband, Philip Iredale, appears in Bucharest as British passport control officer. It is surely reasonable to wonder why so many members of the "Theatre of Youth" cast should turn up in a comparatively unimportant military sector at the same time. However, Mackenzie has a partial defense; Rumania, Bulgaria, and Serbia will serve him as well as any other area in bringing out what he wants to say about the effects of war, so that they have a symbolic or typological function. Bucharest, capital of a country coquetting with the great powers on both sides, and full of suspicion and spies, possesses an odd atmosphere very well rendered. Philip, who refuses Queenie the passport which would enable her to find a haven in England, is a good example of the rigid bureaucrat, who refuses to bend a rule to save a person.

Guy is a representative of a whole generation: he dies young and feels as if he were missing a train. Stella, with her husband dead and her brother apparently dying, is seen by Sylvia as "a woman . . . beholding the society in which she had lived falling to pieces. . . ." "Everybody is dying," she says. "Those who survive this war will really have been granted a second life and will have to begin all over again like children — or lunatics." Very little military action is described in the novel, but Mackenzie has caught such characteristic twentieth-century scenes as the lines of refugees moving away from an advancing army. One vignette preserves the horror for us: "A child was sucking the raw head of a hen; it happened that Sylvia knocked against it in her hurry, whereupon the child grabbed the morsel of blood and mud, snarling at her like a famished hound."

Sylvia and Michael is an early example of the postwar literature of disillusionment; but the narrative has a happy ending; the disillusionment is not complete. In fact, Sylvia's quest is successful in two ways: besides finding someone to whom she can devote her life and who will sustain her in turn, she finds spiritual serenity. The decisive moment occurs when she enters a church in Bucharest and makes a confession, thus resuming the practice of the religion into which she was baptized as a child. Put together, the statements on religion would give the impression that this is the novel's major theme; however, it is often lost sight of. We are given comparatively little insight into Sylvia's religious development, and her conversion is not prepared for.

On the other hand, the general lack of spiritual awareness is emphasized as the cause of civilization's decay. Guy tells Sylvia that the great historical tragedy of the war will be the Englishman's loss of his personality; earlier, religion and individualism have been connected by Sylvia in her argument with Philip. He is as bitter an opponent of religion at the end of his life as he was years earlier; she tries to convince him that life is not a series of rules but a series of exceptions, and she relates his refusal of a passport to Queenie to an inadequate concept of the value of the individual vis-à-vis the state. An enormous soldiers' brothel in Rumania takes on symbolic significance for her: it reflects the Promethean or satanic activity of the modern state, cynically contemptuous of the women whom it degrades. Consequently, Sylvia in her adventures takes on a saint-like quality; in the midst of one of the greatest disasters ever to afflict the human race, she is trying to keep alive faith and hope and respect for the human person.

Still Mackenzie fails to heed Stendhal's warning that a writer who wishes to express important ideas should practice the art of understatement and try to get them by unnoticed; Stendhal's own novels owe their vigor and clarity to their strenuously disciplined expression of personal themes.[28] When a character in *Sylvia Scarlett* says, "We're queer people, we English. . . . In what other country could an actor be knighted for his trousers or an author for his wife's dowry?" it could be Mackenzie himself speaking. Sylvia is made to voice opinions on nationalism, bureaucracy, Spiritualism, and other topics which are very close to Mackenzie's own views. So she impresses Douglas Goldring as not having a feminine personality at all: "Sylvia is, psychologically, perhaps the most interesting of Mr. Mackenzie's creations when we grasp her secret. For she is not really a woman, but a young man of a type which is the distinctive product of all decadent civilizations."[29] This view of Sylvia does not seem entirely just; she is very feminine in her mothering of Lily and Queenie, in her feeling that she needs a man to rely on, and in her concealment of her love for Michael until he declares his own for her. Yet, by putting so many of his own opinions in her mouth, Mackenzie has left himself open to the charge that his central character's sex is wrong. At one point, she is even thinking of writing a book!

Mackenzie follows another of Stendhal's precepts much more closely — that concerning spontaneity and simplicity of style —[30] but his wartime experience was also partly responsible. In writing ten thousand telegrams, he said, he had learned to prune away excess; they had "emptied the honey from what the *Encyclopaedia Britannica* calls my mellifluous style. Telegram after telegram at nearly two shillings a word had made every adjective an unwarrantable extravagance. I was comforted by the thought that Stendhal had taken the Napoleonic Code as a model for his style. . . ." He went on to say, " . . . I was captivated by Stendhal's way of making his characters express so much of themselves in direct speech."[31] In attempting the same thing himself, he was adopting a method which might be thought more congenial to him (given his stage heritage) than florid Keatsian description.

He comments on the dramatic method himself, while still discussing *Sylvia Scarlett:* "Relying as I do so much on dialogue, I fancy that only readers with a dramatic sense enjoy my novels; they must be able as it were to play all the parts themselves, and so grasp their life. I am not interested in creating characters of such psychological complicacy that pages of patient analysis of human motive are required to present them on the printed page. The writer who does this seldom convinces me that his characters existed outside his own imagination and I am not interested in reading about abstractions to which my own imagination is unable to give flesh and blood."[32] In using scene rather than description and narrative summary he would obviously have fewer occasions to use a mandarin style.

In *Sylvia Scarlett*, Mackenzie was also feeling his way towards his later satiric and comic method. The last Sylvia hears of one British officer during the evacuation of Nish is "his unruffled voice leaving instructions that if some white corduroy riding-breeches which he had been expecting by special courier from Athens should by chance arrive before the Bulgarians they were to follow him." There are some good hits at British senior officers who are unable to read anything not written in their own barbaric departmental English and who even have difficulty with that: "The effort even to write 'Concur' represents for the average British general the amount of labour involved by a woman in producing a child. . . ."

There are also a good many comic characters, the best of them perhaps being the wide variety of landladies Sylvia encounters — Mrs. Gainsborough, the most fully developed of these, "once heard a clergyman recite the Spanish Armada, though what it was all about I've completely forgotten." She and many of the other Londoners are Dickensian in conception, though Mackenzie has not Dickens's inexhaustible variety and is going to use someone like her in a number of other novels. The way in which he handles Mrs. Gainsborough also illustrates one of his favorite comic devices: " 'Sylvia!' she suddenly screamed when they were being jostled in the crowded bazaar. 'Look, there's a camel coming toward us! . . . ' " The humor comes from a fat and loquacious lower-class English-woman's being placed in a setting utterly inappropriate for her, such as Morocco, France, or Spain. Mackenzie exploits such incongruities many times in later novels.

For all its merits, *Sylvia Scarlett* is a novel with a number of serious flaws, the worst of them being the coincidences and the rapid and sometimes aimless succession of episodes. Though the first edition of the *Early Adventures* was sold out within a week or so, Erlandson finds that it received fewer and less favorable reviews than any of Mackenzie's novels up to that time; and the reviews of *Sylvia and Michael* were very mixed.[33] In his memoirs Mackenzie categorizes the reviewers of the novel as bone-headed: the critics still thought war should inspire lofty and romantic notions in the mind of a novelist, they were suspicious of a writer who had failed to live up to the label they had affixed to him, and they lacked the dramatic sense essential for an appreciation of his fiction.[34]

Yet his critics' instinct was right; he should have listened to them. The decline of Mackenzie's reputation, Erlandson says, began at this time. It was not so much a question of dissatisfaction with *Sylvia Scarlett* as of puzzlement about what direction its author was taking: "the note of vague disappointment with Mackenzie's general achievement as a writer . . . begins to sound with increasing frequency."[35] The *Observer* described him as "one of the most vivacious and the most unsatisfying of modern novelists." The *Nation* (London) said, " 'Sylvia Scarlett' is entertaining, inventive, sometimes witty. . . . And we say what we do at some length because we had . . . hoped it would be something more." The *New Statesman* summed up this attitude of uneasiness as follows: "After every volume by Mr. Compton Mackenzie since his first, one has looked up and asked perplexedly: What is wrong with this distinguished, graceful, and entertaining writer? He has knowledge, he has charm, he knows how to write; but the reader is not quite convinced. . . . And this new volume leaves one in the same perplexity, asking the same question."[36] The tide had clearly begun to turn.

III   The Vanity Girl

Mackenzie's next novel was a departure from the "Theatre of Youth" series, but he returned to it with *The Vanity Girl*, written in three months in 1919 and published in 1920. The brief notice of it in *Punch's* column "Our Booking Office" describes its nature and indicates the problem it poses:

I should certainly call Mr. COMPTON MACKENZIE our first living expositor of London in fiction. Indeed the precision with which, from his Italian home, he can recapture the aspect and atmosphere of London neighbourhoods is itself an astonishing feat. In *The Vanity Girl* (Cassell) he has happily abandoned the rather breathless manner ·induced by the migratious *Sylvia Scarlett*, and returns to the West Kensington of *Sinister Street*, blended subsequently with that theatrical Bohemia in which *Jenny Pearl* danced her little tragedy. There is something (but by no means all) of the interest of *Carnival* in the new stage story; that the adventures of *Dorothy* lack the compelling charm of her predecessor is inevitable from the difference in temperament of the two heroines and the fact that Mr. MACKENZIE with all his art has been unable to rouse more than dispassionate interest in what is really a study of successful egotism.[37]

How is Mackenzie to build a whole novel around the career of Dorothy Lonsdale? Most of her story was told in the second part of *Sylvia Scarlett*, where she was on tour with Sylvia and Lily Haden in the *Miss Elsie of Chelsea* company. We learned that her real name was Norah Caffyn, and that she had taken Lonsdale from the street on which she lived and Dorothy from her sister — "I suppose in the same way as she used to take her dolls?" Sylvia asked cuttingly. She "possessed a selfishness that almost attained to the dignity of ambition, though never quite, because her conceit would not allow her to state an object in her career for fear of failure; her method was invariably to seize the best of any situation that came along, whether it was a bed, a chair, a potato, or a man. . . ."[38]

In Oxford, Dorothy had the humiliating experience of bringing some undergraduates, including Lord Clarehaven, back to her rooms for tea, only to find Lily sitting on a man's knee; when the three girls were alone again, she burst into a tirade against Lily and slapped her face. In Oxford, she was also selected for the chorus of the Vanity Theatre in London. When Sylvia met her again in London, she thought that Dorothy was principally glad to see her because she was able to talk about lunch at Romano's and supper at the Savoy; and Sylvia rebuked her with "A little less of the Queen of Sheba, if you don't mind." After the meeting Sylvia predicted that Dorothy would marry a lord and would go back on her word and sell her best friend "as readily as a politician will sell his country." The prediction, made to the beautiful dark-haired girl Olive Fanshawe, was completely accurate; when Dorothy announced she was marrying Clarehaven, she met Olive's offer to help her in any way by replying in a voice of ice that "the best way I could help her was by not seeing her any more. . . ."

In fact, Mackenzie's selfish and scheming heroine created a dilemma from which he could not escape. The first half of *The Vanity Girl* is basically an exposure of Dorothy's ruthless ambition. She is handled with considerable irony: "It would be unfair at this stage in Dorothy's career to accuse her of formulating any definite plan to win a coronet, still less of casting her eye upon Lord Clarehaven's coronet in particular; but during these sun-drenched August days she did resolve to do nothing that might spoil the fulfilment of the augury." At one point, while Clarehaven is still trying to make her his mistress and she has shown him the door, she "let her tears go trickling down her cheeks with as much pleasure as a small boy who has found a watering-can on a secluded garden path." When, reversing expectation, the dowager Lady Clarehaven writes a letter pleading on behalf of her son, Dorothy's reply oozes hypocrisy: "I don't think I have ever pretended that I did not love Tony with all my heart, and it was just because I did love him so much that I would not marry him without his mother's consent."

After her marriage, however, the exposure of her faults is no longer Mackenzie's main interest. Her happiness in being a countess is soon qualified by knowledge of her husband's wayward habits. She has sense; he has none. On their first night in the bridal chamber of Clare Court, he begins to talk about his projects: three or four more days there and then they'll be off to the Riviera — " . . . I want to try the pigeons at Monte. After that I thought we'd go to Cairo, or perhaps we might go to Cairo first and take Monte on the way back." She answers, "How can you possibly expect me to go away from this glorious place. . . to tear about the continent with you as if I wasn't your wife at all I don't know."[39] She, the ex-Vanity girl, has affection for his ancestral home and some idea of the responsibilities which a title involves.

Katherine Mansfield, reviewing the novel, paid no attention to the irony of the first part of the story, but used plenty of irony herself in outlining what happens to the marriage:

> Of course, after the usual trouble, she marries him, and is in no time the idol of his family, of the ancient villagers, retainers, and the M̊.F.H. We have a sample of every kind of delicious triumph a young girl from West Kensington could dream of, to Tony in pink silk pyjamas and Dorothy 'in a *deshabille* of peach bloom,' and for background the dark panelled walls. The coming of the child provides a very orgy of emotion. . . . And then the confinement, and the child is born dead, and husband turns gambler and gives up the cards for horses, and loses all, and she finds herself with child again, and this time all is well, and she marries the man who had always loved her and had purchased Clarehaven from her husband. . . .[40]

Satire of Dorothy has been replaced by a "general jamminess and stickiness," in Katherine Mansfield's phrase; and she has not even mentioned that, when Tony banks everything on his horse's winning the Derby and the horse loses, Dorothy offers herself to a sinister Jewish financier named Hausberg in an effort to keep Clare Court, that Tony comes along in the nick of time to horsewhip Hausberg, and that the "happy ending" involves her winning back Clare Court for her son by marrying Hausberg. The novel begins in satire and ends in sentiment.

Yet *Punch* is right in saying that it has interesting aspects. Earlier, Mackenzie sets Mr. Caffyn, who is secretary of the Church of England Purity Society, against Norah's suitor Wilfred Curlew, a reporter with a long, dogmatic chin who writes fierce articles on the condition of modern society for *The Red Lamp:* here the humorous device is so obvious that the result is only mildly amusing. But Mackenzie provides something a little bit unexpected in his description of Lady Clarehaven's two daughters, real aristocrats who don't bother about their appearance: "Arabella's ankles might be slim; but her teeth were large and prominent; her eyes were pale as the wintry sky above them; her hands were knotted and raw; her nose stuck to her face like a piece of mud thrown at a fence; her hair resembled seaweed."

Erlandson is surely right in saying that Mackenzie's aristocrats have affinities with those of P. G. Wodehouse, who in turn perhaps are derived from Edwardian musical comedy, and that they also anticipate Evelyn Waugh's Bright Young Things.[41] Tony's friend Arthur Lonsdale, driving Lily and Sylvia to Brighton in *Sylvia Scarlett* after putting a chimpanzee in Hausberg's flat for Sylvia, is a good example of the mindless playboy: "What do you think the jolly old chimpanzee will do? Probably bite his ear off, what? Topping. Good engine this. We're doing fifty-nine or an unripe sixty. Why does a chicken cross the road? No answer, thank you, this time. . . . "[42] The list of guests at a theater party in *The Vanity Girl* might almost have come out of *Vile Bodies:*

Harry Tufton came, and a Mrs. Foster-French, who went everywhere except where she most wanted to go. . . . The other guests were Captain Archibald Keith, late of the 16th Hussars, who had abandoned the cavalry in order to write the librettos of musical comedies, and a Mrs. Mainwaring, who kept a fashionable hat-shop in Bruton Street and was the widow of poor Dick Mainwaring, a brother of Lord Hughenden. . . . The friends of Mrs. Mainwaring put down any oddness in her behaviour to French creole blood and a childhood in Martinique: to the former was also attributable her *chic* in hats, to the latter the dryness and pallor of her complexion; French blood or French brandy, Martinique or Martell, the Honourable Mrs. Richard Mainwaring certainly did stimulate conversation. . . . But, however jocund her life, her hats were chaste. . . .[43]

Mackenzie's control of tone is not so masterful as Waugh's; his style is too self-conscious, as *certainly, jocund,* and the alliteration and repetition show; still his Edwardian sophisticated society is being observed in a manner similar to that which Huxley, Waugh, and Arlen are going to use to describe the 1920's.

For Katherine Mansfield, however, any possible merits the novel might have had were overwhelmingly offset by Mackenzie's careless flinging of ingredients into the pot and setting it boiling: "In whatever contempt Mr. Mackenzie may hold his public — how is it possible that he should dare to invite them to partake of such sickly food? We should not waste space upon so pretentious and stupid a book were it not that we have believed in his gifts and desire to protest that he should so betray them."[44] The novel was nearly a best seller, but it was sharply attacked by the critics; the heading of a review in the *Observer* summed up the situation: "An Inglorious Success." The *Westminster Gazette* said that the novel "bears upon it every mark of library success: it has every passport to a big circulation; but artistically . . . it does not exist at all: it represents the abandonment of serious intention altogether." The critics believed that Mackenzie had sacrificed artistic integrity for a cheap popular success, writes Erlandson; and his reputation as a serious novelist never quite recovered from the blow.[45]

CHAPTER 5

Mackenzie the Entertainer

I confess that I like a book to be readable; it seems to me that a capacity for entertaining a certain number of people is the chief justification for writing novels. It is a low-browed ambition, but I shall persevere in it myself.[1]

I *Companion Comedies*

Poor Relations (1919), the novel which preceded *The Vanity Girl,* caused an epistolary argument with Thomas E. Wells of Harper's, Mackenzie's American publishers. Wells wrote,

These chapters are no more like Mackenzie than they are like any one of a number of second-grade English and American writers. . . . The writing is commonplace and the reading is dull. . . . The critics will flay the author and the public won't buy the book. Nobody can expect them to . . . Mackenzie ought to be persuaded to chuck this manuscript into the drawer of a desk and forget it. . . . I haven't lowered one bit in my regard for what he has written up to date and I hope to see him go ahead to still greater things. But he cannot expect success with a book like "Poor Relations". He doesn't deserve it.[2]

Delightedly but with no sense of malice, Mackenzie relates how wrong this forecast was:

The book was published at the beginning of October and its circulation in Great Britain and the Colonies was over 30,000 before the year was out. The flaying 'Tommy' Wells prophesied I should receive from the critics on both sides of the Atlantic did not happen. There was not a single bad notice from a British or American paper. I had supposed that all my previous novels showed evidence of plenty of comic invention. Yet apparently my ability to write a novel in which humour predominated came as a surprise, and I was constantly being congratulated by reviewers upon revealing a hitherto unsuspected gift. . . .[3]

But Erlandson has no difficulty in showing that his was a Pyrrhic victory: *Poor Relations* convinced the literary world that Mackenzie was not going to go on to greater things. Douglas Goldring summed up the attitude: "Mr. Mackenzie has found himself — not as a serious novelist, but as that very valuable thing, an entertainer."[4] A dust-jacket summary stresses the humorous quality of the novel:

> *Poor Relations* is Compton Mackenzie in his happier mood. It is, in fact, a farcical comedy, which begins when John Touchwood steps on board the steamship *Murmania* to return to England and ends six months later when he boards the same ship again to sail away from England. John Touchwood is a writer, and after failure as a novelist is at work on a "serious play" based on the life of Joan of Arc. He is also the only prosperous member of his family, and because of a strong inclination to see everything and everybody through rose-coloured spectacles he is mercilessly hounded by a host of "poor relations."
> This is a very funny book indeed, narrated at a brisk pace and enhanced by the author's remarkable power of comic description.[5]

I must confess, however, that I find the novel boring. The "poor relations" who hound John are only slightly amusing — though there is an excellent comic scene in which John has to suffer the intrusion of his brother-in-law, manuscript in hand — "I don't like to interrupt you, my dear fellow. . . . I know you have your own work to consider . . . but I'm anxious for your opinion — in fact I should like to read you my first act." — and has to sit, like a patient in the hands of the dentist, through the reading of this pretentious and fatuous dramatic effusion.[6] But the novel really comes alive only at the end when John decides to elope with his secretary, a girl he has met on the *Murmania* called Miss Hamilton. As if to confirm his switch from passivity to activity, he writes a letter to his family summing them all up and saying in effect (though still with generosity), "You get no more from me." The letter is good — much better than anything which precedes it. And the novel ends neatly with a honeymoon on the *Murmania*. Even so, the character of Miss Hamilton presents a major difficulty. Attractive but mysterious, possessing a will of her own but continually reserving judgment, she exists only as an independent opinion which is hardly ever voiced. But the response to the novel was almost as favorable as Mackenzie claimed. Katherine Mansfield, so ready as we have seen to call *The Vanity Girl* a potboiler, said that the story of John Touchwood's travails "makes the most excellent and amusing reading. The Touchwood family is one of those detestable, fascinating families that we cannot have enough of." In her review, she asserts that Mackenzie's "literary godfathers" were wrong in expecting him to scale the heights, even though "nobly has he repaid that recognition, passing from strength to strength, from intensity to intensity until with his adventures of Sylvia Scarlett, he reached the pitch of high seriousness they had prophesied he should." But in *Poor Relations* "he has descended from his cloudy, thunderous eminence into a valley where we hope he may be tempted to linger. Here, to our thinking, is his proper climate, and here he has every appearance of being most admirably at home. . . ."[7] Alec Waugh put it another way: "Mr. Mackenzie has got over the green sickness." The shadows of *Sinister Street* had been left behind and "the dull adventures of conscientious Michael Fane and unconscionable Sylvia Scarlett have had at least temporary surcease." He recognized *Poor Relations* as "a real achievement in simple comedy."[8] The *New Statesman* made a similar but more definitive estimate: "Mr. Mackenzie started as the hope of the English novel, and he has written a first-rate book for a railway journey. Many a writer who has set out with an ambition no less exalted has come to a far worse end."[9] It seemed that he had found his *métier* as a writer of light entertainments.

Concerning the companion novel *Rich Relatives* (1921), Edward Shanks wrote that "Mr. Compton Mackenzie's new book is so mechanically accurate an inversion of *Poor Relations* that one wonders what interest he can have had in doing it."[10] Just as I disputed the received opinion about the earlier novel, I would like to dispute Shanks's view of the later: it seems to me that *Rich Relatives* is funnier and better. Its heroine, Jasmine Grant, is the daughter of an Italian mother and of a Scottish father who had revolted against the "onward and upward" motto of his family and who had ended his days as a painter on Capri, which Mackenzie calls Sirene. Left an orphan, Jasmine has to move from sunny Italy to a life of cold storage in England, where she is handed on from relative to relative, outraging each family of relatives in turn by her unthinking violations of their stiff conventionality. She early contrasts the "smell of immemorial respectability" in York Minster with the frank odors of candles, perspiration, incense, and garlic in the Duomo of Sirene; in her uncle Sir Hector's summer home at Spaborough, the atmosphere is so deadly that she feels guilty at turning on a tap. Before her, she thinks, "stretched years and years of silent sunlit vacancy, in which she would be walking about on tiptoe and throttling every gush of spontaneous feeling just as she had throttled that bath tap."[11]

Of course she is rescued; Mackenzie uses the Cinderella theme amusingly, even to the extent of having his heroine appear unexpectedly at a ball in a borrowed dress to meet her Prince Charming. Shanks calls the Prince a "dull, tiresome and shadowy young man," which is probably correct. He is merely a convenience; Mackenzie does not take some of the mechanics of his plot very seriously. His real interest is in the gallery of eccentrics whom Jasmine encounters — Lady Grant, condemned by her best feature to confront the world with an attitude of hauteur, since there is nothing she can do with her nose except show it in profile; Aunt Cuckoo, who glides like a ghost and speaks tonelessly; Aunt Ellen, wife of the Dean of Silchester and "sharply aware of the might of a Dean, because that might was mainly exercised by her"; the Dean himself, who, with head bent over his work, gives the impression that someone has left a large ostrich egg on a desk; Aunt Mildred, whose loosely fitting false teeth give her a continual sound of eating; and so on.

It is obvious that Mackenzie is tagging these characters in the Dickensian fashion with eccentric habits or physical peculiarities which make them easily identifiable; but they are sufficiently amusing and Jasmine's encounters with them sufficiently varied and lively for the novel to carry the reader along. Jasmine's foreign upbringing is used to throw their oddities into perspective; it is also used to highlight the oddity of many things which Englishmen take for granted: "Incomprehensible country, where ices were found in sweet-shops, and where sweet-shops were closed on Sunday! Jasmine gave it up. However, they did find a sweet-shop open, where she ate what tasted like a pat of butter frozen in an old box of soap, cost fourpence, and was called a vanilla ice-cream."[12]

The theme of English narrowness, respectability, and provincialism was hardly new; Mackenzie's friend Norman Douglas had used it in *South Wind* only four years before *Rich Relatives*. Mackenzie's grotesques are, however, more sinister than Douglas's; they are as sinister as similar grotesques can be in Dickens. In the penultimate chapter of the novel, Jasmine is living with Sir Hector and Lady Grant in Harley Street and is thinking that "if a famous prisoner, he of Chillon or any other, had been invited to change his outlook with her own, he would soon have begged to be put back in his dungeon." This reflection is not humorous; the persecution to which Jasmine has been subjected has produced the kind of nervous distortion of the imagination which conceives of Harley Street doctors as poisoners in the Chamber of Horrors. Sir Hector's waiting room becomes "curiously symbolical of the kind of imprisonment to which madness subjects the human soul." Cinderella's escape, therefore, is from a grotesque world which she can no longer regard with amusement because it tortures her and tries to deprive her of hope. The novel is something more than a pleasant trifle for a railway journey.

Kenneth Young appraises the complexity of the novel admirably; Shanks, missing it entirely, wrote, " . . . Mr. Mackenzie is surely not yet as near the end of his invention as he seems to represent himself."[13] The opinion that Mackenzie was wasting his time on trifles was becoming widespread. Mackenzie relates that, when F. Scott Fitzgerald visited him on Capri in 1925, "He reproached me for disappointing my admirers by writing books merely meant to make people laugh." The rejoinder was "that the greatest writer in the English language had not considered it beneath his dignity to make people laugh with plays like *The Comedy of Errors.*" After this statement Mackenzie delivered a counterattack: "It's time you produced another Mark Twain in America."[14] He considered the writing of comic novels to be a more skillful and demanding occupation than most people realize; and this position he consistently maintained and defended.

Still he did not confine himself to this mode, nor did he choose it as his special *métier.* At the end of World War I, however, he had recognized the need for some profound change in his manner of life and writing. Evidently he considered that psychological embroidery had taken the place of simple incident in fiction, and for this new fad he had an aversion; the paragraph in which he discusses the matter is obscure, but it seems as if he felt that he would have to withdraw from any attempt to compete in the new manner.[15] He may have been depressed by suddenly finding himself as no longer a coming writer but one whom the modern movement had passed by. But, as we have seen, his depression of spirits produced comic novels — not indecision or inertia. In a letter to John Peale Bishop, Fitzgerald wrote, "We're just back from Capri where I sat up . . . half the night talking to my old idol Compton Mackenzie. . . . I found him cordial, attractive and pleasantly mundane. You get no sense from him that [he] feels his work has gone to pieces. He's not pompous about his present output. I think he's just tired. The war wrecked him as it did Wells and many of that generation."[16] Fitzgerald's concluding judgment has an element of truth; but, tired or not, during the 1920's Mackenzie changed islands several times, founded *The Gramophone,* and wrote fourteen novels.

II   *Varied Approaches*

These novels provided eloquent testimony to his versatility. Two were spy stories set in the Mediterranean during World War I; two dealt with capers on Capri; another was set on an island off the coast of Cornwall, and another on the island in the South Seas; and three of them were combined into a very ambitious religious trilogy. The variety of themes should have proved that Mackenzie had not lost his power of invention. True, he did repeat himself: his own Kensington boyhood provides the initial setting for many of his novels, and the cottage at Beech Farm, Alton, Hampshire, which his family bought when he was thirteen suggested the "Galton" and environs which come into *Sylvia Scarlett, The Heavenly Ladder,* and *Buttercups and Daisies.* True, he often boiled the pot, relied too much on coincidence, and finished off his novels carelessly.

Still, a great deal more effort went into the novels than might be thought. Whenever he took up something, he went at it wholeheartedly; this was true of his gardening in Cornwall and his gramophone collecting when he was living in the Channel Islands, and it was equally true with the subjects of his novels. The religious trilogy contained an astonishing amount of precise detail about the Anglo-Catholic element in the Church of England; much of this information came from memory, but he also tells us that the writing "involved a good deal of reading to check my ecclesiastical facts."[17] For *The Old Men of the Sea* (1924), he read the *North Atlantic Pilot,* the *South Atlantic Pilot,* and the *Pacific Pilot,* and had the satisfaction of having a ship's captain express surprise that he had been his own navigator: he had his nautical details right.[18]

This last novel of course reflected one of Mackenzie's obsessions — islands. When it was republished under the title *Paradise for Sale* (1963), Mackenzie related in a foreword that he had heard in 1919 that Sunday Island, the largest of the Kermadec group some six hundred miles off New Zealand, had been abandoned after an eruption, and that he had played with the idea of taking out a party of pioneers to resettle it. He found out, however, that the island had already been granted to a New Zealander; and he settled for Herm and Jethou instead, traveling to the South Seas only in imagination. His narrative was based on a true story told him by his friend Hope-Johnstone

"about some rogues who had persuaded a number of credulous people to embark for a mythical paradise in a ship which they scuppered
at the mouth of the Thames, getting safely away with the money they
had extracted from their dupes."[19]

The summary of the novel at the front of the Macdonald edition
stresses two points in Mackenzie's use of this real-life story: none of
the voyagers really anticipate that the expedition will be anything but
a swindle; and, in a manner of speaking, they have already arrived at
their destination from the first moment of departure: "All of them,
villain and gull alike, had at least gained access to the private worlds
of their own imaginations." The "I" of the story, Marsham, suc-
cumbs to the lure of adventure even though he knows that the South
Sea Settlement Co., whose advertisement has attracted his friend
Briscoe, is a sham and a fraud.

As so often in reading a Mackenzie novel, we wish that when
Mackenzie was launched on a congenial theme he had treated it with
respect. He wrote the novel, he tells us in a Foreword, because he
needed a thousand pounds to start *The Gramophone,* and he wrote it
in six weeks. The result was wild-eyed romanticism. The number of
violent deaths in the course of the voyage prepares us for something
truly horrendous when the destination is reached, but that something
turns out far in excess of possible expectations. It involves the
bizarre operations of nemesis on an old man named Hawkyard,
scalded to death for love of gold; and the destruction of two others by
volcanic action when "a wave rose up out of the sea all of a sudden,
and come down on them from above, and fire come up from un-
derneath, and there was nothing left of the ship nor the crew that
sailed her. . . ."[20] This catastrophic event is reminiscent of the
providential toppling of a statue in Bulwer Lytton's *The Last Days
of Pompeii;* as always when Mackenzie uses his Bulwer Lytton
effect, we wish he had thought of a better way out of his plotting
complications.

The title of *Fairy Gold* (1926), published two years later, suggests
Celtic mist and moonshine, and this *Evening Standard* serial indeed
possesses plenty of both. But again Mackenzie has drawn on his own
experiences and introduced a characteristic theme. He had been
forced to sell the lease of Herm to Sir Percival Perry, who had made
a fortune after the war out of scrap iron bought from the government
for a fraction of its value.[21] Mackenzie merely moves his island to the
other end of the English channel, off Cornwall, and changes his
profiteer's name to Sir Caleb Fuller. With sanctimonious hypocrisy,

Sir Caleb thinks he is doing the islanders a favor by destroying their way of life — putting in paved roads, establishing a golf course, and even bringing over an army tank he happens to own to carry seaweed in. ". . . . I *am* so hoping that we are going to be able to turn dear little Roon into one great big boatload of happiness," he beams. By now it has become apparent that the clash of cultures has become one of Mackenzie's favorite themes and that in this struggle he will always take the side of the underdog; he takes great delight here in repelling Sir Caleb from Roon's shores. Earlier Mackenzie has taken equal delight in showing an inflexible military autocracy baffled and discomfited by the idiosyncratic islanders. But this story is only a warm-up for what he is going to do later in a number of novels set in the Hebrides.

Extremes Meet (1928) shows him using some of his earlier characters and settings with a good deal of skill in this spy story set in an unnamed Mediterranean city (presumably Athens) during the Great War; the country is neutral, but its king is friendly to Germany. The central character is the fairly disreputable naval officer Waterlow, whose main desire is to get a ship; but he has blotted his copy book, and he is considered too fond of drink. As we see him, he is a conscientious intelligence officer who is plagued by fools in the military and diplomatic services. He is unmarried and has a mother living in Hampshire; the Galton (Alton) scene is always at the back of his mind — the image of a peaceful rural England which knows nothing of such matters as those he is involved in.

The story deals with Waterlow's exploitation of a girl in order to try to trap a German major and a German submarine. The girl is Queenie Walters, Sylvia Scarlett's friend; she is still trying to get away from Zozo, she is still seeking refuge in England, and she is promised a passport by Waterlow if she will help him trap Major von Rangel. His plan fails, but the novel ends almost happily with him being given command of a ship. But by this time he has realized what he has done. Earlier, he has looked at Queenie, "a pale gold birchen leaf tossed hither and thither by the winds of war," and has felt some compunction at the way he is going to use her; yet he has put this reluctance aside as a kind of sentimentality which will not do in war.

Before the end of the novel, Waterlow has gained in moral understanding: "The fortune of war had so far given him nothing to reproach himself with, except his treatment of this girl babbling away beside him. . . . Nothing but this slim golden girl on his conscience? Yet that was enough, when one stopped to think what it meant to violate a girl's personality as he had deliberately done and then cold-bloodedly planned to send a lot of human beings to death as a result of the outrage."[22] He could probably have found a defense for the latter action, since he was trying to destroy a killer submarine, but for the former there was no defense; in this tightly knit novel, Mackenzie gives a striking example of a particular type of moral cowardice which he finds pervasive in the modern world.

These novels suffice as examples of the minor fiction which Mackenzie produced in the 1920's and indeed in subsequent decades. They were written by a novelist who, as Fitzgerald said, was not pompous about his output and would, in fact, think of himself as a craftsman turning out a useful product. Indeed, he was never simply arranging counters in predictably acceptable patterns. His writing was always related to a serious view of life; out of deep conviction, he attacked the bureaucrats, the profiteers, the inhibitors of personal freedom, the personal representatives or impersonal advancing tentacles of megalopolis or cosmopolis.

III   *Erratic Manners and Morals*

Two novels of the late 1920's call for special consideration, however, as do several later ones which are predominately satiric, in which Mackenzie rises well above the level of mere competence. Mackenzie wrote these two novels, *Vestal Fire* (1927) and *Extraordinary Women* (1928), in the *South Wind* vein. The debt to Norman Douglas is obvious in them, and the second is dedicated to him — "for it was you who sent me to Sirene by the magic of your conversation so dearly enjoyed among the fogs of London fifteen years ago." As in *South Wind,* the island is seen as a place where eccentricity flourishes[23] — Douglas has his Miss Wilberforce, an outwardly proper Britisher who sheds her clothes and her inhibitions when inebriated, and Mackenzie has a parallel figure in Effie Macadam, who changes from a tiresome little woman into a Sirene "character." When Mackenzie writes, "And on that shady terrace you expanded," he is echoing the note which sounds throughout *South Wind,* in which the island of Nepenthe is a place of mental and spiritual enlargement. Douglas's hedonistic message is heard only intermittently in *Vestal Fire,* but when Nigel Dawson says, "I think you ought to do exactly what you want. I think everybody ought to do what he wants," we discern the authentic *South Wind* moral attitude.

There are many other resemblances — the effects of the island on a clergyman's outlook; the description of the operations of Italian justice; the warfare between neighboring municipalities over their patron saints (together with saints' legends and religious processions which degenerate into farce); the description of deputations which ought to be, like Caesar's wife, above suspicion, but turn out to be collections of reprobates; and above all the wild Bacchanalian revels. There are major differences, however, in intention and style. At least five characters in *South Wind* join Douglas in the zealous preaching of evil ways; V. S. Pritchett writes of him, "Compared to Anatole France, he's a dominie."[24] Mackenzie preaches no sermons in his two novels. Also, if he employs some of Douglas's urbane sophistication and irony, they are considerably toned down; and the note of pathos or sentimentality which Douglas tries to banish by his *carpe diem* philosophy comes in strongly, especially in *Vestal Fire*.

This novel deals with actual persons and events; in fact, Mackenzie had to postpone writing it during the war because "the story was developing so dramatically that I knew I must wait for its end in real life."[25] When he began writing it, he made a false start with forty pages which had to be destroyed. This was an unusual thing for him to do, and it emphasized the difficulty which the theme gave him — he was obviously much more concerned about matters of form than Douglas, who was never really a novelist. One of his problems came from the fact that the two old ladies on whom the book centered had to be made neither ridiculous nor improbable; furthermore, they were Americans, and had to be given American speech and habits.

An additional problem was that of telling a scandalous tale without giving offense; he decided the best thing to do was to treat the scandalous aspect comically: "When I made the comic aspect of my theme in *Vestal Fire* predominant I was not intending to satirize homosexuality. I was merely trying to deprive what was called an 'unpleasant' theme of any 'unpleasant' appeal."[26] An additional problem was that of introducing forty characters into the first fifty pages without confusing the reader. Mackenzie decided to avoid scene painting for its own sake; he would describe no scene which did not provide an immediate background for some character, and he relied upon being able to suggest the total atmosphere by the accumulated effect of dozens of snapshots. He also calls attention to the symmetry of the novel; it is divided into three parts, each of eight chapters and each of the same length (the first being a mere three pages shorter and the third, three pages longer than the second). He was modeling himself on Douglas, but he was not going to make his novel the *mélange* or *potpourri* that *South Wind* was.

The vestals of the title, Maimie and Virginia Pepworth-Norton (two cousins who have adopted the same name), came to Sirene on a visit and decided to stay. Their Villa Amabile became famous for its hospitality; it possessed the shady terrace on which guests expanded: "You expanded physically owing to the amount you had eaten and drunk, but thanks to the classic beauty of the scene and the Sirenian conversation . . . you expanded in many other directions as well. . . . You looked up at the conical hill of Tiberius on the summit of which, a thousand feet up, you saw the yawning cellars of what had been his mightiest residence, and muttering over to yourself as many lines as you could remember of Shelley's sonnet on Ozymandias you bowed your head before the triumph of time and sipped your whisky."[27]

Into this atmosphere of serene contentment comes Count Marsac, who quickly becomes a special favorite of the two dear ladies. Sirene society welcomes him as they do, in spite of some questionable behavior on his part; but, when it is learned that he has been convicted of a morals offense in France, Sirene society is much harsher than the two American cousins. They will hear no evil about the Count, and those who come to them with evidence of it are shown the door and sent insulting letters of excommunication: "After what you had the impudence to come and say this afternoon please understand that we do not wish to see your painted face inside our house again. . . . "

The controversy about Count Marsac is fanned by two amused observers, Duncan Maxwell (who is Norman Douglas) and John Scudamore, a scholar who is trying to rehabilitate Tiberius; in view of Douglas's own homosexuality, it is interesting to hear Maxwell berating Marsac: "He stinks like an unwrapped mummy of stale spice. I've no patience with these soulful pederasts. Everything must be turned into a blasted religion, that's what makes me so furious." But the fires of indignation at Marsac's ill-treatment continue to burn in Maimie and Virginia over the course of the years, surviving the banishment of the Count from Sirene; a four-year period during which he wanders through the East and becomes devoted to opium; an expedition to the East on which they accompany him; and his failure to match patriotic sentiments with action during the Great War. Only after Maimie has died as a result of a traffic accident in Rome does the moment come when Virginia turns on the Count and says, "You've lied to us all these years."

Mackenzie has not much patience with Marsac: "Carlyle once said that Herbert Spencer was the most unending ass in Christendom. He had not met the Count." On the other hand, the novel contains a whole gallery of rich and varied personalities, many of whom are identified in Douglas's *Looking Back: An Autobiographical Excursion.* Some of these are working at their obsessions with singular devotion: "There was an American translating Goethe, an Englishman translating the sonnets of Hérédia, and another Englishman wrestling with Mallarmé's *L'Après-midi d'un Faune.* . . . There was a German writing a history of the Saracens, and there was John Scudamore, an American, who was amassing the material for a history of Roman morals." "When these authors met in Zampone's Cafe," Mackenzie comments satirically, "they always enquired most warmly after one another's pregnancies before each began to talk exclusively about his own."[28]

Scudamore, "a tall thin man with a long fine beard and a skin unnaturally white," accumulates more notes on the Romans by the year, but every year finds that it would be more presumptuous to begin writing. Joseph Rutger Neave, the most indomitable egotist of all this lot, "could hitch the wagon of any conversation to the star of Dante," even though Maxwell insists that "he simply takes a geographical interest in Hell because he thinks he'll get there one day." In Maxwell himself we discern one of the most notable literary portraits of the eccentric, erudite Douglas: "Laughter enveloped him in a cloud through which his small deep-set eyes came glittering like two stars. He was of a florid complexion with a long tip-tilted sliced-off pragmatical nose such as you may see in any number of portraits of eighteenth-century Lowland lairds; but his magnificent vitality instead of exhausting itself in a struggle with agriculture, and his subtle mind instead of wasting itself on the split straws and dusty chaff of Presbyterian theology, had been allowed to swell and ripen in the sun. . . ."[29] This quotation is only part of a long portrait suffused with affection.

Maxwell is constantly on the go — always hurrying away to collect arrowheads on the top of Monte Ventoso or snakes in Bavaria. Affectionately as he is portrayed, however, he is not a major character in the story. The two fiery vestals, who are of central importance, are treated with sympathetic comedy. There are many ironic aspects in the relationship between them and Marsac — as when the two ladies present this notorious pederast with an illuminated poem in a little gilded frame, "Because You're You," or when Virginia thanks him for a novel slandering most of his acquaintances on Sirene and ending with a tornado of invective against women: "We were so pleased to receive your lovely book and read that sweet and dear dedication to our selves. . . ."

But, whatever their failings, they are regarded with admiration.

Their story is set in a long perspective of time: "They are dead now — Miss Virginia with her ivory eagle's countenance and eternally fluttering fan, Miss Maimie with her tight intolerant mouth and high cheekbones, her defiant smouldering eyes and her Quaker air. The Villa Amabile stands like a vast wedding-cake that has turned grey and dingy in a shop-window. . . ."[30] "They brought with them the puritan fire of old America," Mackenzie says in summation, "and quenched it in the pagan earth of ancient Europe." So he lets them recede from his tale, and gives us only a brief glimpse of a new postwar Sirene become so blasé that the most outrageous statements of the futurist Marinetti produce not the slightest ripple of shock.

Mackenzie relates that he had trouble publishing *Vestal Fire:* "Even the gay spirit of the twittering 'twenties was not yet tuned up to publish a novel which, though it laughed at some aspects of it, admitted frankly that homosexuality existed,"[31] But the difficulty with this novel was slight compared with that over the next: "I cannot remember when I finished *Extraordinary Women;* what I recall was the disagreeable shock of hearing from Newman Flower that he was not prepared to risk publishing it, and a week or two later that George Doran was equally shy. The future of *Extraordinary Women* was solved by Martin Secker's arranging to publish a limited edition of two thousand at a guinea."[32] The difficulty arose simply from the fact that his women *were* extraordinary; his subject was lesbianism. That his publishers had reason for concern was shown by the suppression of Radclyffe Hall's *The Well of Loneliness* for its daring treatment of the same theme just before *Extraordinary Women* was due to appear. According to Mackenzie, the attack on Miss Hall's novel was launched by James Douglas, editor of the *Sunday Express,* who declared that he would sooner give a healthy boy or girl a dose of prussic acid than a copy of this book.[33]

When *Extraordinary Women* appeared, its prosecution was discussed but decided against by the Home Office — almost to Mackenzie's regret, it would appear, since he intended to conduct his own defense and, as he told one official, "You robbed the public of many good laughs. I should have enjoyed cross-examining you."[34] There was considerable discussion at the time about why Mackenzie got away with it and Radclyffe Hall did not. The answer becomes apparent in Kathleen Nott's review of a recent republication of *The Well of Loneliness* — the one is a tract and the other is not: "I object to the publishers' description — 'The classic novel of Lesbian love' — for the book is highly romantic. And, alas, to be 'classic' about sex, either straight or bent, you have to be detached and on the dry side, and either sadly paradoxical or cruelly funny. So that not only does Dante seem nearer to psychological reality than Miss Radclyffe Hall, but also Compton Mackenzie with his Capri queers."[35] In her survey of *Sex Variant Women in Literature,* Jeannette Foster comes to a similar conclusion about the impression given by Mackenzie's story: it seems to be "the report of a witty and superior observer" and its total effect "is one of cool detachment."[36] For this reason, his book was not repressed.

As with *Vestal Fire,* Mackenzie emphasizes the difficulty of composition; in fact, he calls *Extraordinary Women* the most exhausting book he ever wrote.[37] Robertson thinks that he handled the variations on his theme with just the right touch: "In the delicate artistry of its construction, and the lightness of touch with which the note of airy persiflage is sustained throughout the work, one is constantly reminded . . . of 'The Rape of the Lock'. The manner is entirely adequate to the matter and exactly catches the frivolous tone of the leisured, shallow, pampered, social set at which its mockery is aimed." And the writer is so completely unimpassioned that he is like an entomologist with a collection of exotic, brilliantly colored butterflies.[38] We can accept this judgment with only a few reservations; only very occasionally is there a failure of tone.

On our first view of her, Rosalba Donsante is being told by her Swiss grandmother that she looks too much like a man; and she is accepting the statement as a compliment. A beautiful schemer, she has two women in tow — square-jawed Rory Freemantle, who breeds French bulldogs and promotes female boxing matches, and soft, tearful Countess Giulia Monforte. Giulia is soon to respond to the call of duty — her husband is ill — and disappear from the scene; Rory, who envisages the possibility of a final and permanent friendship with another woman, is to pursue Rosalba to the end of the novel — and become her slave and her dupe.

In Rosalba we have an intriguing study of a female Don Juan who considers herself invincible in love, and for whom every other woman of Sapphic temperament (and some without it) represents a challenge. We see her welcomed on Sirene like a reigning monarch, and she immediately discards both Rory and Giulia to captivate a sixteen-year-old girl named Lulu de Randan. When Lulu's mother comes along, she captivates her as well. There is a succession of others, including a musician from the Midi called Cléo Gazay and an American named Janet Royle, until she meets her match in Olimpia

Leigh. All the others are shallow; Olimpia is not. A famous musician and composer, she is not to be won by tactful letters, gifts, and compliments as the others were. Yet she is intrigued by Rosalba's beauty, and for a while both play the maiden loth with each other, until finally Olimpia turns on her and accuses Rosalba of stupid and erratic behavior.

Through all of these affairs that Rosalba has, Rory watches and waits; and her greatest happiness consists of remodeling her villa as a home for Rosalba and herself and in persuading Rosalba to spend a quiet month there with her. But, when Rosalba goes so far as to announce that a theft at Olimpia's villa was committed by Rory, this accusation is the last straw for all her friends — except for the faithful Rory. Even she is finally disillusioned when Rosalba continues her vain pursuit of Olimpia: "A grand passion," thinks Rory, "had turned into a bad headache." But Rory meets her situation, ironically, with stiff British resolution; and the novel closes with her having tea in her villa with a young man characterized by his nickname, Daffodil.

There are marvelous comic scenes in the novel — Rosalba and Lulu on a moonlight drive up the winding road to Anasirene, with Lulu's governess Miss Chimbley pursuing in another carriage, and Rory and Giulia in a third; one woman with a monocle (Rory) seated at a café table and confiding to another woman with a monocle (Countess de Randan) the history of an unfortunate love affair, and becoming so emotional that she drops her monocle into her grenadine; Rosalba's dinner parties, with eight women sitting round a table, "the palpitations of whose hidden jealousies, baffled desires and wounded vanities was . . . as potent as the dreadful mustering of subterranean fires before an eruption"; Rory's housewarming, with its baffling mixture of unisexual and bisexual emotions and with a young man named Hewetson giving a rendition of Bacchic frenzy dressed in nothing but a pink handkerchief and a paper rose; and the investigation of Olimpia's robbery by a *maresciallo* of police who has to transcribe into his notebook such un-Italian details as the name of her birthplace: Schenectady.

A great deal of the comedy comes from Rosalba herself: she is absurd and does not realize it. Even though she was modeled on a real person, she is reminiscent of the title figure in Max Beerbohm's *Zuleika Dobson*. "We have noted her lack of humour, her capacity for intrigue, her childish vanity, her egoism, and her insincerity," writes Mackenzie — all descriptions that would apply equally to

Zuleika. When Zuleika sits listening to the Duke of Dorset playing the piano, she keeps time with her fan — the only one in the audience not moved by his performance; afterwards, she not only makes but repeats the trite comment, "I don't know anything about music really, but I know what I like."[39] Similarly Rosalba listens impatiently while her current love, Cléo, plays the piano in a Roman salon: "Oh, why did Cléo choose such long pieces . . . ? . . . Five minutes. Ten minutes. . . . A quarter of an hour. . . . Rosalba muttered viciously inside herself. . . . "[40] Like Zuleika, Rosalba is the epitome of the second-rate except for her beautiful appearance. Stung by the serpent-tongued Principessa Buonograzia — "Forget about Olimpia as she has already forgotten you. . . . A small flea can perhaps disturb a beautiful dream, but it is the flea who is forgotten" — she attempts a dignified withdrawal from the dining room of the Hotel Augusto, but it is marred and mocked by her ungrammatical English: " . . . I will not lower myself to eat no more with you because I would choke myself with disgust for your vulgarity." Of course, Zuleika is not the victim of the crowning insult which the resentful Cléo throws at Rosalba: "You are normal."

Mackenzie does not satirize lesbianism so much as the backbiting, jealousy, intrigue, selfishness, and self-deception which accompany it. Nearly all his women are shallow; Olimpia is the main exception. As I have said, his handling of his social butterflies is very deft; however, after about a hundred pages of Rosalba's emotional entanglements, he suddenly seems to become tired of following her. In the space of a few pages, he introduces a number of plotting complications, and he intrudes some sententious comments of his own about normal and abnormal love affairs. Eventually, the light and lambent irony of the early pages returns; with exceptions allowed for, the control of tone is remarkable. Mackenzie is urbane, but not cynical; mildly disapproving, but never denunciatory; unsparing in his exposure of folly, yet compassionate towards the foolish. The figures he sets into his Sirenian landscape have their pathetic as well as their ludicrous aspects.

CHAPTER 6

The Four Winds of Love

I *The Plan of a Magnum Opus*

IN the spring of 1926, Mackenzie gave a *Daily Mail* reporter an outline of a huge novel in seven volumes to be called *Our Seven Selves*. It would be a million words long; it would begin in 1897 and end in the 1920's; and it would deal with man's self-determination in relationship to profession, woman, family, class, country, humanity, and finally God. He indicated that he had other equally grandiose schemes in mind, including a history of the Crusades in eight volumes, and an ancestral epic in thirty volumes (starting in the year 1000) which would be the amusement of his old age! Presumably, if he had found his publishers enthusiastic, he would have begun his mammoth novel as soon as possible; for it he needed two years free of financial pressure — a blessed state he was not to know for several decades. By mid-1928, he was considering putting his service career to factual rather than fictional use: "I felt that the only way to use my war experiences was by putting them down on paper as a true story."[1] So he began *Gallipoli Memories,* and *Our Seven Selves* went into limbo.

Yet the plan of a long chronicle novel stayed with him, and when he mentioned the title *The Four Winds of Love* to Newman Flower of Cassell's in 1932, Flower's reply was encouraging: "I hope you are going to make the novel a long one. It is time we had a long serious novel from you. When I say this, I don't cast reflection on the lighter books which, as you know, I like very much, but I think you have also a serious public which now needs a little attention."[2]

Mackenzie's answer that *The Four Winds* was intended to be very long was almost supererogatory. "As circumstances would rule," he wrote later, *"The East Wind of Love"* would not be published until 1937 and *The North Wind of Love* would not blow until 1945. The long novel of 200,000 words would become a rather longer novel of nearly a million words."[3] As the work grew, Flower became more and more worried about its bulk; and the correspondence given in Octave Seven relates a complicated story of misunderstandings and disagreements leading to a final break. (Rich and Cowan published the first two volumes; Chatto and Windus, the remainder.) Flower later conceded, in thanking Mackenzie for dedicating the second volume to him, "Of course I was all damnwrong. . . ."[4] But, of course, he was dead right. And unfortunately the extreme length of the work (plus its interruption for *The Windsor Tapestry*) kept Mackenzie from finishing it before World War II began and forced its publication to extend over an eight-year period.

It is clear that Mackenzie thought of *The Four Winds* as a very serious and ambitious work, "the *Sinister Street* of my middle age. . . ."[5] Some reviewers of the first volume felt that it would restore his critical reputation. "When the race is over," declared the *Evening Standard,* "Mr. Mackenzie . . . will have achieved his masterpiece."[6] The *Daily Mail* said, "He has given us no comparable work of the imagination since he wrote *"Sinister Street"* more than twenty years ago, and in scope and insight, as well as in the quality of the experience communicated, it surpasses that young man's masterpiece."[7] If it is a masterpiece, it is a neglected one; does it deserve more serious consideration than it has received? Leo Robertson, who views it as "by far his greatest work," maintains that "the full measure of his achievement as the author of it has yet to be taken."[8] Similarly Kenneth Young writes that it must be regarded as Mackenzie's *chef d'oeuvre* in fiction.[9]

But, on the other hand, it has had severe criticism from the first. In *The Tablet,* Derek Traversi observed that the undertaking was a little too vast for Mackenzie, "who is one of those writers in whom fluency has always tended to outrun genuine distinction." In the absence of a coherent and individual vision, he thought, the author's remarkable assembly of detail tended to fall into a meaningless catalogue.[10] Perhaps the most devastating attack was by Cuthbert Wright in another Catholic periodical, *Commonweal,* in 1946: "The onetime lover of some of Mr. Mackenzie's early books, in attempting to tackle, as a whole or in separate units, "The Four Winds of Love" is subjected to an experience almost of esthetic despair. He has to call up every resource of nostalgia and sentiment to write of it with the maximum of charity and the minimum of exasperation."[11] Wright then ticked off the indictments against it which he had listed in reviews of the earlier volumes — length, diffuseness, boring characters, a rich overripe Keatsian vocabulary. He objected especially to the style: ". . . Mr. Mackenzie has never guarded his prose, because he has always completely lacked self-discipline, and has made up in a kind of romantic exuberance for what he lacks in definite quality."

Was it merely romantic exuberance which caused Mackenzie to make the work so long? With Flower's pressure to keep it short and his awareness (expressed in the preface) that the longer he made it the more unpopular he would be with the critics, why did he persist in his folly? The answer is suggested in Octave Five of his autobiography, where he apologizes for repeating much of what he has already said in his war memoirs: "Critics who accuse me of a lack of selectivity must believe me when I assure them that from the very beginning of *My Life and Times* I have continuously refused to give my memory a loose rein. I have tried to keep every year as it came along as much in the mood of that year as if I had kept a diary."[12] This is exactly his intention in *The Four Winds* — to convey as exactly as possible what it was like to live in 1914, or 1915, or 1920 — to make the reader experience the emotions aroused by the election of 1906 or the suffragette movement or the question of Irish independence.

In giving a panorama of Europe in his times, he used Byron's *Don Juan* for a model; he said he read and reread it. Byron, however, was more mocking towards his hero; Mackenzie, more closely identified with his hero's position. Yet he consistently maintained that the novel is not concealed autobiography; he is not John Ogilvie, though the two of them share many similar experiences. Mackenzie was never the drifter his central character was; Ogilvie is slow to develop passionate convictions and to act on them. Presumably Mackenzie is trying to capture the tone of a life, or of most lives: there are times when Ogilvie is carried along by the mood of a period, and at other times he revolts against what he considers general barbarism. As his life proceeds, he does develop a greater sense of purpose. But year by year he is intended to reflect the main preoccupations of Western Europe, to act as a mirror of his age.

II *The Theme and its Development*

The main theme is announced early. *The East Wind of Love* opens with a debate at St. James's School on Home Rule for Ireland. A Blimpish politician, Colonel Yarborough, sounds a call for national unity in a time of trouble (it is the period of a British Vietnam, the Boer War): "England cannot afford for even one schoolboy to express what at a time like this I do not hesitate to call opinions subversive of patriotism and disloyal to the great Queen whose subjects we are proud to be." After him an Irish member of Parliament — not a stage Irishman but a small man with a trim dark beard — rises to put the case for Irish independence in entirely convincing terms. A schoolfellow of Ogilvie's, Edward Fitzgerald, then denounces England with such savagery that the audience reverts to its ingrained hostility to Ireland. He is answered by a precocious Jewish boy, Emil Stern, who makes a brilliant speech on a Joycean theme — Ireland is a beldame who waits by the fireside dreaming of her youth; she has contributed nothing to humanity. Fitzgerald and Stern remain important figures in the story, and so do their concerns — justice for oppressed nations or racial groups. John Ogilvie, who is of Scottish descent, soon becomes involved in the Jacobite question and the movement for Scottish independence. In one way and another, *The Four Winds* brings in a remarkable number of persecuted or inhibited minorities — Poles, Greeks, Czechs, and even Bretons and Cornishmen.

Beginning at the time it does, the book is also bound to ask what is to follow Victorianism. Like Byron, Mackenzie has abuses to condemn, especially the survival of hidebound ways of doing things; but the story he tells is mainly that of the supersession of the bad by the worse. His main complaints are absence of principle and of statesmanship; he tells of the drift from expedient to expedient, and therefore from crisis to crisis, by political leaders who are too ignorant to put contemporary events in historical perspective. John Ogilvie does develop such a perspective; concerning any place he visits in his travels, he is likely to enquire, "What did it mean in the past, and what does it say to the present?" Entering a church in Cracow, he finds himself "absorbed into seven hundred years of prayer, lost like a grain of corn in this vast granary of human aspirations." Suddenly from a tower of the church a trumpeter sounds the hour:

That tune had been blown half-way through the thirteenth century to warn the city that the Tartar hordes were at hand. An arrow had pierced the watchman's throat before his tune was finished, and ever since, without missing an hour of the day or night, trumpeter after trumpeter had blown that same tune from the four windows of that room at the top of the church tower

and ever since had ended on the same wavering note, the last note blown by
the watchman before the Tartar arrow pierced his throat. Eastward the
trumpeters had blown defiance to the Tartar, and southward they had
blown defiance to the Turk. To the west they had proclaimed that Poland
was the guardian of Europe against Mahomet and to the north they had
given warning that she stood firm against Luther.[13]

A medieval church and a thirteenth-century event have, therefore,
continuing significance in the present. Characteristically, Mackenzie
picks as a symbol of achievement a nation — Poland — more often
in subjection than not, and a trumpet blast which ends in a quaver:
"Its strength was in the feeble wavering note at the end. Its triumph
was its failure."[14]

In contrast, the clock of St. James's School "stared blandly and
benevolently" and "beamed with the complacency of ordered time,"
thereby testifying to the comfortable assumption that the British
Empire is the best solution yet found to the problems of the world.
John's school is, therefore, a foretaste of the world which modern
man has created, "the self-complacent conservatism which had
dragged its huge unwieldy saurian body and button-head from the
steaming marshes of Victorianism into the present."[15] The twentieth
century begins, and Victoria dies; but, from his father's platitudes
about the need for "a sane, a courageous, and a genuinely
progressive Liberalism," John gains the impression that everything
remains marmoreal and unchanged. And, when change does come, it
is not always for the better.

When the tale resumes in *The South Wind* (1937), the action occurs eleven years after the first volume; and John has been to Oxford
and become a successful playwright. Still, as he explains to his
mother confessor Miriam Stern, he looks back on his youth as an
orchard of blossom which never produced fruit. Not surprisingly,
therefore, he is exultant at the beginning of the Great War; he looks
on it as a crusade: "One had criticized England, principally, I think,
because one had come to think of England in terms of party politicians and the popular Press, but when the country responded to that
call from Belgium criticism was forgotten. All that monstrous exploitation of Ireland in the interest of party politics, all that hideous
and brutal treatment of women over the agitation for the vote, every
black memory vanished when we entered a war from motives as near
to generosity as could be imagined."[16]

His war is as exciting as Mackenzie's own; but, two years later, his
enthusiasm has disappeared — he is tired of risking men's lives to

obtain information which is never used because of blundering stupidity. Eventually, he comes to see the war as the ultimate exploitation of the individual; and this factor is brought home to him forcibly when he invades the island domain of a courteous elderly gentleman named Chrysomali, who is a German sympathizer: "Now in my own island where I am surrounded by a few people who look up to me as the father of a family, I am at the mercy of this fever which has seized the world. My family has enjoyed power in its day. I want nothing except my flocks and my vineyards and my corn and the fish in the sea round my island. . . . "[17] In the name of hypocritical promises, all such islands of tranquility are being destroyed. "Surely when we sacrifice to patriotism," says one of the characters, "we sacrifice the best part of ourselves."[18]

On other romantic islands, Ogilvie meets Euphrosyne Ladas, who seems to him the spirit of Greece, and a beautiful girl half his age, Zoe Gadrilakis, to whom he becomes engaged. Zoe is real, her death aboard a torpedoed ship is too contrived, and John's grief for her is too literary. But Mackenzie captures very convincingly the excitement of dangerous escapades, the sense of expectation when a major attack is made and the desolateness when it fails, and the bureaucratic muddle which surrounds all military enterprises. *The South Wind,* then, deals with both the romance and the antiromance of war.

Ogilvie's romantic involvement in *The West Wind* (1940) is with Athene Langridge, an American who is the wife of a rich dilettante named Wacey. She is fairly convincing, and the attraction she has for John is real enough, but the affair is conducted in trite terms with heavy reliance on moonshine and starshine. Wacey's mother is real enough too — "In her grey travelling-cape she seemed to annihilate the future with the pervasiveness of a creeping sea-fog" — but the plot relies too heavily on accident and coincidence, especially when divorce proceedings are rendered unnecessary by Wacey's convenient death. But, if John finds one kind of fulfillment in a happy marriage, he has not otherwise found himself. The war has not produced a new burst of creative energy in him; it is "as sterile mentally as a game of golf," and the only drama to be extracted from it is its destructive effect on the personality. He is forced to agree with Fitzgerald's criticism of him: "What's the good of your bloody plays? There's nothing behind them."

In contrast, Emil Stern has found a faith, Communism; he is so strongly dedicated to human perfectibility that he is willing to sacrifice humanity to it. John at least retains his respect for individuality; in an era dominated by dour-looking men who have made fortunes out of poison gas, and bumptious Wellsian figures who proclaim that Squandermania will put the country on its feet, he prizes the gallery of eccentrics, figures out of a rich past, which London can still display, such as Mrs. Sayers the porter's wife: "I don't hold with these Americans myself. We had one of them in Queensberry Mansions six months back. Nasty n'ya-n'ya way of talking. 'Your voice wants oiling,' I said to him once when he was trying to teach me my own business. I reckon this President Wilson is another Knowall. Just another Kayser if you ask me. . . . "[19] The priceless thing Mackenzie learned from Wells, he said, was to write Cockney dialogue; and Mrs. Sayers is a good example of his skill in doing so.[20]

West to North (1940) shows the shift of John Ogilvie's interest to Scotland. It opens with his living in Cornwall with Athene and his beginning to feel that he is too happy and too unconcerned about the problems of the world. In an era of volcanic change, these issues are sufficiently obvious: the British Government, while preaching self-determination of nations at Versailles, sends the Black and Tans to put down the Irish; the Poles fight the Bolsheviks for their lives; Ogilvie's beloved Greece remains in a state of chaos; and in Italy the rise of Fascism begins. At a meeting of the Nationalist group in Edinburgh, John explains what the war has taught him: rival imperialisms must end by destroying one another, and the peace and happiness of the world depend on the breaking up of these power structures.

One line of the story follows the troubles in Ireland, which are presented most movingly with the murder of Fitzgerald's wife and eventually the murder of Fitzgerald himself in circumstances he had foretold. Because of his friend's death, John becomes a Catholic — believing in supernatural reality, apparently, because of Fitzgerald's premonition. But most of the religious discussion at this time is by Julius Stern, Emil's brother, a convert of many years' standing; John alludes now and then to religion, but he is chiefly occupied with political questions; and the process of conversion which one would expect to be dealt with in detail in such a long life story is not really presented at all. The point of view behind it is made clear in *The North Wind,* however: ". . . he had waited to weave religious and political conviction together with a single gesture of faith. A spiritual imperialism and internationalism was to blend with a political nationalism expressed by many small states."[21]

In *The North Wind* (2 vols., 1944 - 45), Ogilvie is involved, sometimes seriously and sometimes farcically, with various Scottish Nationalist organizations. Anticipating history, one of these plots the capture of the Stone of Scone, the Stone of Destiny on which the kings of England have been crowned ever since it was brought from Scotland by Edward I in 1296. The plot eventually fails — unlike that in 1950, when the stone was spirited out of Westminster Abbey and returned briefly to Scotland. Scottish nationalism may seem only a cranky cause, but Ogilvie has an explanation for its appeal to the young: "They want a background. They feel lost in the vastness of a modern imperialistic State."[22] In *West to North,* Ogilvie has made use of a favorite metaphor of Mackenzie's to condemn metropolitanism and urbanization; it is "a sign of humanity's surrender to the advantage of the swarm. . . ." The *Four Winds* is a protest against depersonalization; Mackenzie wants a political community small enough for the individual to feel that he has some voice in its affairs.

The *North Wind* also deals with the deterioration of the international situation in the 1930's. A trip to Poland with Julius enables Ogilvie to take the pulse of Europe. When their ship stops at Kiel, their view of it provokes a ritual condemnation of Germany: the buildings are mean, the people are meaner, the sky is dirty gray, dirty gray is the color of the nation's soul. They dock at the uncanny toy town of Gdynia, the Polish port established because of the internationalization of Danzig; and they see its inhabitants as "like the people of a city conjured into abrupt existence by sorcery, and liable to dissolve at the whim of the magician responsible for their being." Yet they find the inhabitants of Cracow envying Gdynia's modernity; visiting Poland is like visiting the beating heart of Europe, but John has no feeling that Europe is listening to its beating heart. At the end of the novel, while a gay rondo of Beethoven's is being played, John thinks back over his whole life and suddenly shudders: he is thinking of the rondo of death which the younger generation is facing.

The place of the smaller nations in John's vision is clear enough. While he is in Ireland, Mackenzie writes, "And round the house the west wind boomed and roared, blowing towards Europe." Joyce viewed Ireland as a sow which ate its farrow, or as batlike, cut off from the source of light — Europe. Mackenzie sees Ireland as a fount of inexhaustible Western life; the special function of the Celt in the modern world is to prevent cosmopolitanism from making individuals insignificant. His view of imperialism is similar to that of Forster in *Howards End,* as Ernst Schlegel explains it to his nephew:

". . . your Pan-Germanism is no more imaginative than is our Imperialism over here [in England]. It is the vice of a vulgar mind to be thrilled by bigness, to think that a thousand square miles are a thousand times more wonderful than one square mile, and that a million square miles are almost the same as heaven. That is not imagination. No, it kills it. When their poets over here try to celebrate bigness they are dead at once, and naturally. Your poets too are dying, your philosophers, your musicians, to whom Europe has listened for two hundred years. Gone. Gone with the little courts that nurtured them. . . ."[23]

Or it is similar to the view expressed by J. M. Synge in the preface to *The Playboy of the Western World,* where he described his good fortune to encounter in the west of Ireland a people whose imagination and language were rich and living: "In Ireland, for a few years more, we have a popular imagination that is fiery, and magnificent, and tender; so that those of us who wish to write start with a chance that is not given to writers in places where the spring-time of the local life has been forgotten, and the harvest is a memory only, and the straw has been turned into bricks."[24]

Mackenzie does not want to turn his back on Europe; his Julius Stern, who is sympathetically presented, stresses the necessity of being in contact with the heart of Europe if he is going to express the emotional state of his time.[25] Like T. S. Eliot in *Notes Towards a Definition of Culture,* Mackenzie can see virtue in a common culture and the subsidiary cultures that contribute to it. While he desires a system of spiritual values commonly held, he would like to see political structures kept small enough to be meaningful to ordinary people. Relating contemporary chaos to the sick soul of modern man, he seeks, like Synge, places where springtime has not been forgotten. His search resembles that of D. H. Lawrence for men not yet destroyed by technology and industrialism; however, there are differences: ". . . David Rayner the novelist once sent me a picture-postcard of Monte Cassino to say that the place was rotten with the past. He was one of those self-tormented introverts who are increasing faster and faster under modern conditions and who, I suppose, feel a grudge against the past for their own thwarted existence in the present."[26] Rayner is Lawrence; and, in contrast to him, Mackenzie sees the need of combating modern rootlessness by inculcating in man both a response to nature and a reverence for the past.

In the conclusion of *The Four Winds of Love,* the symmetry of John Ogilvie's life is completed when, after the death of Athene, he returns to the Mediterranean island of Lipsia, meets Euphrosyne Ladas again, and marries her — like a Ulysses returning, after years of wandering, to his Penelope. Despite its length, the novel is carefully designed; all the winds have their symbolic meanings and correspondences with Ogilvie's emotional life and responses to human problems. As Robertson shows, it is not primarily a love story: elements of romance enter into John Ogilvie's life as into most; but, when Mackenzie employs the symbolism of the Four Winds, he understands by love something much wider and deeper than ordinary romantic love: "He seems to mean by it nothing less than that most fundamental urge in individuals to reach out from their ego-centres in order to find fulfilment of themselves. . . . It is, indeed, the natural outward movement of the whole spirit of man in its quest for self-realisation ultimately to be found only in other selves and through them in God."[27] Listening to Beethoven's Sonata in F Major at the end of the book, John thinks how the tempos correspond to the stages and moods of his own life. His thoughts during the rondo, as we have seen, are somber — "It was turning into a rondo of death as I thought about man's attempt to live without God." Yet he is not dispirited; if this era is no longer one of faith, it remains for him an age of hope and love.

III   *Evaluation*

The novel therefore deals with an important theme which is carefully worked out. Yet the plot has its weaknesses, and again we are forced to believe that Mackenzie learned the wrong things from Hardy, such as the overuse of coincidence and the summary dismissal of characters when they become inconveniences to the plot. As to characters, there are some interesting major ones such as Miriam Stern (despite Cuthbert Wright's animadversions against them), and a whole host of fascinating minor ones — sometimes they are given real personalities, even though they appear only briefly. On the other hand, some characters are merely types; Geoffrey Noel, who is based on Norman Douglas, is reduced to a few characteristic concerns, such as homosexuality and worry over money. The style has its infelicities: Mackenzie is still too fond of words like *tralucent*. But the worst fault of all is the trite emotional response which is likely to accompany one of the thousand references to music: " 'You know, Emil, when I hear somebody like that kid playing as she played this afternoon, I get an absolute conviction that there must be something beyond this life,' John declared."[28]

There is, however, a great deal of vigorous writing, especially of a satiric tone; for there is nothing "middlebrow," in Cyril Connolly's sense,[29] about passages like this: "at the General Election the voters all over Great Britain returned to hysteria and made themselves safe for ultimate disaster by electing the first 'National' Government, a red, white, and blue chimera with the swollen body and gouty legs of a Conservative, the head of a Labour renegade on which the cap of liberty had turned into a cockscomb, the fawning tail of a Liberal renegade, and the plumage of a goose believed to be capable of laying golden eggs if trodden in low water by bankers."[30]

Nevertheless, the novel must be judged an ambitious failure. As Young notes, the volumes are not stylistically all of a piece: "the earlier ones dealing with schooldays, early loves, Irish nationalist friends and the war in the eastern Mediterranean are narration — with superb dialogue up to and beyond the best in *Carnival* or *Sinister Street;* the later ones, written after the outbreak of a new world war, are overcast with a sense of 'that misused past.' "[31] Young finds the change of pace convincing: with advancing years, Ogilvie and his friends become more ruminative. But, as "that kid playing as she played this afternoon" illustrates, some of Ogilvie's opinions are banal or eccentric. When he decides to abjure violence in the cause of Scottish Nationalism, we wonder how he could ever have contemplated it in the first place; when he thinks that the removal of the Stone of Scone may almost bring down the Empire, we wonder why he doesn't foresee what actually did occur when the Stone was spirited out of Westminster Abbey — that it would be treated as a very amusing practical joke.

Traversi is wrong in saying that Mackenzie lacks a coherent and individual vision, but he is right in criticizing the quality of Ogilvie's responses: "The truth is that Ogilvie's surface brilliance covers an undeniable poverty of outlook. He is ready to express himself, with a confident flow of well-shaped sentences, upon practically any topic; but where his deeper feelings are concerned, his reactions reveal, beneath the slightly unctuous ease of their expression, a notable conventionality. The opening of *La Traviata,* seen by him at

Naples, inspires him to banal comment: 'Hush, the prelude is beginning, and I must surrender to thoughts of tears and roses, of sweet champagne and young love.' "[32]

Again, there is a greater depth to Ogilvie's personality than this criticism suggests; there are things unsaid, which are sometimes more important than things said. But, if we are to feel history as it occurs, we must follow John Ogilvie's perspective; and, as Traversi shows, there are times when we stop short and refuse to follow him. *The Four Winds* is, in places, a considerable achievement; because of its delineation of the violent and conflicting emotions surrounding such *causes célèbres* as the Irish question, it will remain a useful record of the times with which it deals. Yet it must remain a matter of regret that, when Mackenzie had begun writing his *magnum opus,* he felt it necessary to lay it aside — that the quixotic streak in him made him take up the cudgels for the Duke of Windsor. But, if Mackenzie had ever found it possible *not* to come to the defense of an underdog, he would never have been the man he was.

CHAPTER 7

Satires on the Anthill and the Hive

A traditional function of the writer of fiction has been to throw new light on questions of the day through imaginative treatment of them. Jonathan Swift ridicules the absurd predictions of the astrologer Partridge by foretelling the death of Partridge — and he follows it, at the appointed time, by an account of Partridge's sad ending; or he assumes the role of a Dublin drapier to oppose the patent given William Wood by the British Government to mint copper coins for Ireland. Charles Dickens hears accounts of the mistreatment of boys in Yorkshire schools, goes there himself to investigate, and writes *Nicholas Nickleby.* Upton Sinclair attacks the Chicago meat-packing industry in *The Jungle;* Frank Norris, the operations of grain speculators in *The Pit;* Sinclair Lewis, the philanthropic medical foundations in *Arrowsmith.* Now fiction seems to be surrendering this function to the documentary, yet it is safe to say that novels like George Orwell's *Animal Farm* and *Nineteen Eighty-four* will always have a greater impact than books like Truman Capote's *In Cold Blood.*

Mackenzie displayed a remarkable ability to turn today's headlines into tomorrow's novels. After being prosecuted under the Official Secrets Act and escaping with a mild fine and a strong rebuke, he satirized the British intelligence service in *Water on the Brain* (1933). His contribution to wartime economy measures was another satire, *The Red Tapeworm* (1941), which sardonically suggested that any governmental measures to prevent waste would be sure to cause it. When the sea serpent in Loch Ness was very much in the news, he invented a second sea serpent, *The Rival Monster* (1952). When the British government announced plans to establish a rocket range in the Hebrides, he voiced his wrath in letters to the *Times* but subdued it sufficiently to write a very funny novel, *Rockets Galore* (1957). And, when the first sputnik went up, he wrote *The Lunatic Republic* (1959).

I   *Cloak-and-dagger Lunatics*

In dedicating *Water on the Brain* to Principal Rait of Glasgow University, Mackenzie referred to his own ability to transmute passionate concern with a contentious issue into humorous fiction. This novel, he admitted, had its source in a recent disagreeable experience of his own; but he claimed that in writing about it he turned annoyance into something akin to pleasure. *"Water on the Brain,"* he wrote, "represents my own amusement at the end of it all. It is the friendliest archery, and not a shaft has been barbed with malice or poisoned by vexation of spirit." But to take a lenient view of institutionalized stupidity was difficult: "the mercy one may show to individuals cannot always be extended to a system, and although *Water on the Brain* is a deliberate caricature of Intelligence there are features in the system which will be recognized even by those with a great deal less humour and knowledge than yourself."

In his autobiography, he is also able to take a fairly light-hearted view of the matter; he makes it appear that cloak-and-dagger lunatics were making a mountain out of a molehill. He had some great moments of fun at the judicial hearing, as when the Attorney-General was impressing upon the judge the great danger of Mackenzie's informing the world who "C" was (Sir Mansfield Cumming, Chief of the Secret Service during the war) and Mackenzie produced the information that "C" had been dead for over ten years, or when it was revealed that another former Intelligence officer had actually revealed his own connection with the service in *Who's Who*. Yet the matter was serious enough, as a distinguished solicitor, Sir Reginald Poole, emphasized: "If you plead not guilty, you can call those witnesses from Athens and Constantinople and the case could go on for two or three weeks and cost you £15,000 or more. . . . And then the Judge might send you to Wormwood Scrubs [a prison] for nine months — not a pleasant experience — and the public would think that you must have done something dreadful to get such a sentence. And as the case will be heard *in camera* you won't be able to tell the public about it because it is contempt of court to say what happened *in camera*."[1] Sir Reginald was able to arrange with the Attorney General that, if Mackenzie pleaded guilty, a fine of £500 would be imposed; even that was reduced, to £100, after General Hamilton and Admiral Sells had testified to the defendant's character and services to his country.

The *Times* commented on the case in a leading article: "It is clear from the Judge's observations that in the present case the prosecution did not press too strongly their view of the harm which was actually caused. The purpose of the action was, perhaps, rather to warn those 'whose urge to write is greater than their discretion.' Mr. Mackenzie is not the first, and might not otherwise have been the last, to err without intention against the Statute. It is a doubly welcome exercise of judicial leniency which has saved Mr. Mackenzie from gaol."[2] It testifies to Mackenzie's sense of humor that he was able to write a comic novel about a case which might have brought him a prison sentence.

The novel, however, is not so funny or so successful as it might have been. Mackenzie does make humorous use of initials — "N" and "P," chiefs of different branches of Intelligence, may never be referred to by their real names, though everyone knows them. He also gets the two branches working against each other and thoroughly muddled in their operations, but he does so only by straining coincidence to the utmost. His central character, Major Arthur Blenkinsop, is invited to become a secret agent because of his knowledge of a Central European country called Mendacia; working with the usual *femme fatale* of such stories, Mme. Renata Tekta, he contributes indirectly to the restoration of the monarchy in Mendacia. But only the Intelligence Service could construe the preparations for this restoration as connected with a rising in Scotland. The novel closes with the Service receiving an almost fatal shock: by incredible coincidence, the name of its headquarters has been used in a spy thriller. Naturally, the headquarters has to be moved:

Pomona Lodge is now an asylum for the servants of bureaucracy who have been driven mad in the service of their country. Only the other day the chronicler was privileged to be shown over it by one of the most distinguished alienists of the day, and it will be long before he forgets the experience. There he saw distracted typists typing away feverishly at reports which would never be read even in eternity. There he saw worn-out servants of the Inland Revenue assessing their own nurses' incomes at fabulous amounts. There cheek by jowl sat the squandermaniac and the suicidal junior clerk — the one writing out cheques for trillions of pounds, the other collecting the odd bits of red tape of which he hoped one day to weave a rope to hang himself.[3]

This satire is perhaps modeled on Swift's Academy of Projectors, and it would not be unworthy of that great master of satire himself.

Many a reader of *Water on the Brain* must have said that this mixture of farce and absurdity could not have given an accurate picture of British intelligence work; but the Philby case proved it did. In their investigation into the career of this famous double agent, the London *Sunday Times* "Insight" team made it clear that the ineptitude of the British Secret Service had made his career possible — especially the rivalry between M. I. 5 and M. I. 6 (which became the Secret Intelligence Service after World War I; Sir Mansfield Cumming, "C", had been its first head). The truth was as strange as fiction, Mackenzie's fiction; in fact, the man who recruited Philby for the Secret Service appeared as a character in Mackenzie's novel.[4] It would be rash to say that the British did not win the intelligence battle over the Germans in World War II; but, at the same time, the evidence produced in 1967 substantiated what Mackenzie had been saying about the bureaucratic ineptitude of the British Secret Service for fifty years.

II *The Ministry of Waste*

The Red Tapeworm (1941) was also the product of annoyance: "I had decided that the best way to allay the irritation through the waste of paper by the Civil Service, the Royal Navy, the Army and the Royal Air Force was to write a funny novel about the Civil Service."[5] Mackenzie has wartime conditions in mind; but, as the opening shows, he deliberately avoids specific mention of them: "At a quarter to nine on a fine evening in the late autumn of a year when the country was still outwardly at peace the newly-appointed Minister of Waste alighted from his car at Broadcasting House. He was to address the nation at nine-fifteen."[6] The Minister's broadcast, in which he announces a crusade against waste and declares, "I want your rags. I want your bones. Yes, I even want your old bottles," begins a chain of hilarious consequences.

Instead of having the Ministry submerged by a flood of refuse from all over the country, however, Mackenzie concentrates on the response from a small place called Hodford. An erratic lady named Miss Quekett wishes to donate six china chamber pots decorated with smeared mottoes like "Your Country Needs You"; and, when she cannot see the Minister, she starts hurling them at Oliver Huffam, the Minister's Principal Private Secretary. A truckload of scrap iron collected by "Six Grateful Listeners" has to be redirected to a dump near where it came from. Lady Lavinia, the Minister's wife, calls up irately to get someone to collect a bath, a birdcage, a baby carriage, and miscellaneous other items which have been left at her house in Eaton Square. The crusade has been launched, of course, without any arrangements for collecting the waste, without any idea of its possible use — that is in the hands of the Experimental Department — and without the issuance of the promised twenty million copies of pamphlet MW 4560/45 hx/731 with accompanying buff, pink, and pale green forms, which, when filled in by the recipients, would be sent to the District Controllers, who would then issue white forms A, B, C and D on which owners and gatherers of waste would make application for it to be removed. "These District Controllers," Mackenzie tells us, "had been busy for some months in advising the Area Controllers to advise the Zonal Controllers to advise the Regional Controllers to advise the Ministry of Waste to acquire some of the best agricultural land in the country, in order to provide great waste dumps all over Britain."[7]

In the absence of the completion of these procedures, three objects — a bathtub with a hole in it, an incredibly filthy three-burner paraffin stove, and a baby carriage "from a grateful mother whose tots are tots no longer but fine young men ready to serve King and Country when the call comes" — go back and forth between Hodford, the Ministry, Eaton Square, and Oliver Huffam's house in Chillingham Gardens; no matter how ingeniously they are disposed of, they seem fated to return. An additional complication comes from a territorial dispute between Regional Controllers in Scotland; and, when Oliver is sent to deal with it and coincidentally the baby carriage is delivered to his house, his wife Gertrude is ready to believe the worst. While he is in Scotland, he learns with dismay that the Minister is to give another broadcast — this time, in the Children's Hour; the extent of his suffering while he listens to another plea for action by a politician who is so rash as to give his own home address drives Oliver to take the first drink between meals he has ever had in his life. The children of England respond magnificently; the Minister's house is filled with old boots, old horseshoes, and postcards.

The children of Hodford, urged on by Miss Quekett, arrive at the Ministry with a truckload of rubbish, and are directed by a sardonic doorman to Eaton Square. But this is only a delegation, and the Minister can handle delegations with the utmost aplomb; he thanks the children, instructs them to build a neat dump with the very valuable waste material they have collected, and tells them it will be collected in a few days, or perhaps a few weeks. But hardly has this delegation left when two Boy Scouts appear with the impossible bath and the incredible stove. "My God!" cries Lady Lavinia in horror. "They've come back!" This time the Principal Private Secretary takes the necessary action; having been informed by the Regional Controller for the Highlands and Islands that he has a waste reserve ready, Huffam sends the offending articles to Scotland. It is entirely fitting that in the next New Year's Honours List he should be made a Companion of the Bath.

The Minister, Mr. Apsley Howe, is a stock figure — a self-important, plump little man always worried about the effect of an action on his constituents; so is his wife Lavinia — concerned chiefly about who is going to win the next important race and looking something like a chestnut mare herself. The Permanent Secretary, Sir Oliver Huntbath, epitomizes the intention of the Civil Service to subdue whatever party may happen to be in power; "Sir Claud is anxious to see you sir," says Huffam to the Minister after the latter's broadcast to the children — "in the tones of an assistant-master telling one of his pupils that all his efforts have been in vain and that the Headmaster now has the matter in his own hands."

But the Red Tapeworm, Huffam himself, is the real triumph of humorous characterization:

Besides being tall he was very thin, with red hair and the dead-white skin that sometimes accompanies such hair. If some men are born Civil Servants, some achieve Civil Service, and some have Civil Service thrust upon them, Oliver Huffam belonged to the first category. No other calling was imaginable for him. His boyhood had been marked by a devotion to rules, a zest for superfluous information, and a most praiseworthy diligence for the prescribed task. He never dreamed of becoming an orchid-hunter in Borneo or a log-roller in Canada or an explorer of the Never Never Land in Australia.[8]

Before leaving a load of rubbish at a garbage dump, he makes a list of the deposited items for filing and future reference; before giving the baby carriage away to someone who needs it, he consults the Solicitor of the Disposals Board; and in the twinkling of an eye he can produce a memorandum to fit any contingency: "Until householders have received the special forms issued notifying District Controllers that agglomerations of waste material have been accumulated pending further instructions to be received as to the disposal of such agglomerations in conformity with the instructions as to same issued by the Ministry of Waste to Regional, Zonal and

Area Controllers for the purpose of transmission to District Controllers and communicated by them to the general public through the medium of advertisements inserted by the Ministry in both the national and local newspapers. . . ." He really *believes* in the webs of complication which he spins: "These people who denounced red tape did not have the job of cleaning up the mess when the red tape was cut through. Red Tape, White Behaviour, and Blue Water, that was the British Empire, and each of the three was indispensable to its lasting might and glory."

Combining farcical action and farcical characters, and bringing things together neatly at the end, Mackenzie makes *The Red Tapeworm* a very effective satire. It is noteworthy that he avoids overdoing things; instead of preaching his point, he lets it become apparent through the actions and speeches of the characters. This novel is deftly contrived and executed.

III   *Moonmugs*

When Mackenzie based a novel on space exploration some years later, he again attacked bureaucracy and its implications. *The Lunatic Republic* (1959) describes an intriguing voyage in the future. In 1997, under the sponsorship of the Celestial Chinese Republic, a rocket containing a Chinese scientist named Tin Pan and an English commercial traveler named John Bosworth landed on the moon. They discovered that the barren wilderness which we see from Earth was caused by a nuclear war which had taken place three thousand years before between two peoples when each had been determined to preserve its own way of life. A small tract on the other side of the moon survived the holocaust, and here the Lunatic Republic carries on the manner of existence for which man, in Mackenzie's view, seems heading.

The moon creatures, men hardly four feet high with blue faces, all look exactly alike; they are all dressed in close-fitting blue breeches and blue shirts with collars open at the neck; and on the front of their shirts they carry numbers like those of motor cars: "Pup 301," "Dad 333," and so on. They talk Basic English; *mug* is *man* and *wug* is *woman,* and from these come masculine compounds such as *bookmug, digmug, doormug,* and *ritemug* (secretary), and feminine such as *cookwug.* There is no need for watches; A-time begins when everybody on Lunamania wakes up at the same moment, B-time, when everybody sits down to First Eat; F-time, when everybody watches the gimpers (athletes) at their sports; G-time, when everybody talks about what they saw in F-time; H-time, when everybody looks at television (which the Lunatics call *see-all*). The inhabitants of Lunatic City all live in great hives which tower into a synthetic sky. There are nine hundred and nine of these hives, each of them with nine hundred and ninety cells. In Mackenzie's society the ultimate in conformity has been reached: everyone looks the same as everyone else, everyone does the same as everyone else at a given time, everyone lives in the same sort of cell, and the small number of names in use makes it necessary for a person's name to be supplemented with an identifying numeral.

The attack on bureaucracy continues in this novel with a satiric forecast of the situation which the use of paper in government offices will eventually produce: "At last there were no trees and no paper left at all, and although a suitable substitute was discovered on which official reports could be written, it was too expensive a product to be used for toilet-paper, and laws were passed both in Lunaria and Lunatia making constipation compulsory."[9] The device of the imaginary voyage enables Mackenzie to present, in exaggerated form, the movement he sees in mankind's affairs towards the mass and away from the individual. Associated with this, of course, is a constriction of humanity; and, in relation to it, the use of Basic English is as important as Newspeak is for Orwell; the means of expression the Lunatics employ give us a vivid impression of their almost sub-human mentality.[10] The loose structure of the novel enables Mackenzie to set forth his own opinions concerning current affairs with sometimes unfortunate effect, but the novel as a whole is a clear expression of the opinion Bosworth expresses to Tin Pan in a discussion of what progress means: "It makes me much more sad when I think that never again will the world have a Homer or a Shakespeare or even a Burns or a Catullus to sing, that all your sublime Chinese art will belong to the past, and that man made in the likeness of God will turn to the likeness of a white or a red or a black ant."[11] *The Lunatic Republic,* then, is one skirmish in Mackenzie's long battle with the ant-hill or the hive.

Mackenzie has always been ready to tilt a lance at officialdom. Besides the examples already given, many others might be cited. In 1961, he wrote the novel *Mezzotint* that deals with race relations on a Carribean island which is a British Crown Colony. The theme is stated by Maurice Florimond, one of the descendants of the original French planters — that it is the same story everywhere with colored people: "We have taken their land in Africa, we have carried them away as slaves to the New World, we have emancipated them from slavery but we want to keep them in a permanent state of inferiority to ourselves."[12] The Negroes are another example, then, of the oppressed groups with whom Mackenzie so often sides. In the fictional situation described in this novel, the Frenchmen, the "grands blancs," are in the position of privilege; but the stupidity of the Colonial Office helps keep them there. A mezzotint of Stoke Poges churchyard presented to a new school by the British Council is perhaps symbolic of British unimaginativeness. The plot hinges on the arrival of a new Governor, George Clapshaw, who causes a furore by appointing an octoroon as acting Attorney-General; there are a good many comic complications in this novel, but it is ultimately serious and unsettling because it presents no easy solutions.

Several of these satiric novels — such as *Water on the Brain* and a later attack on the Civil Service, *Paper Lives* (1966) — are perhaps only routine broadsides, but one of them, *The Red Tapeworm,* is very successful both as comedy and as satire. As we have observed, Mackenzie has used a considerable variety of literary techniques in them; one was an imaginary voyage and antiutopia; one gave a near-realistic description (mingled with a certain amount of fantasy) of an actual situation; several treated actual situations in frankly farcical and exaggerated terms. The technique of reducing something to absurdity was evident in all of them, but the means of pointing out absurdity varied from novel to novel: no handy formula would cover all of them. In the small percentage of his output which we have discussed in this chapter, Mackenzie demonstrated enough comic inventiveness to make the name of many a novelist; as we shall see, when he found a vigorous and vital society to defend against the busy bees and intrepid ants, he was even more successful.

CHAPTER 8

Living off the Map

I N Octave Six of his memoirs, Mackenzie describes how he became involved with Scottish nationalism, thinking of it not so much as a territorial idea as a spiritual one — a protest of free individuals against the growth of serfdom: "A growing complacency in servitude is the most conspicuous effect of the machine upon the mind of man."[1] He also tells of the Nationalists' putting R. B. Cunninghame Graham forward as their candidate for the rectorship of Glasgow University in 1928 and of their great surprise when he came only sixty-six votes behind Stanley Baldwin in the election. Outlining Graham's position, Mackenzie describes his own: "He looked at the future of Scotland with that logical Latin mind, and faced up to the fact that unless Europe could preserve the independence of her small nations Europe was doomed."[2] Behind what may seem mere quixotry and romantic medievalism, therefore, lay a serious questioning of the drift of the contemporary world.

Because of his passionate enthusiasm for this cause, Mackenzie decided to leave Jethou and move to Scotland. He tells with delight of living for a time on Eilean Aigas, an island in the middle of the River Beauly in Invernessshire and the home of Lord Lovat, head of the Fraser family. Using it as a base, Mackenzie was able to acquaint himself with the life of the great Highland clans and their chiefs. Later, he moved to the island of Barra in the Outer Hebrides, and he built a house on it in 1935. In a broadcast, which he delivered in 1936 under the title "Living off the Map," he described the way of life he found there. "Barra is an extraordinarily happy place," he said. "Laughter is the keynote. There is always a good story going the rounds. Gaelic is a great language for wit, and with three-quarters of the population of Barra speaking both Gaelic and English, the native Gaelic wit salts the English."

Nine visitors out of ten, he went on, when asked how they were enjoying their stay on the island, replied not with praise of the scenery but of the people. He found a remarkably cosmopolitan outlook among them, an extremely pleasant combination of shyness with good manners and *savoir faire*. They were all individuals; the real pleasure of life on Barra was that of "living intimately in a small community which is a microcosm of the great world, with one important difference, however, and that is that everybody in it is a real person; the way that life *on* the map is moving just now does make it more and more difficult for people to be themselves."[3]

The Scottish setting came into *The Red Tapeworm;* so did one of Mackenzie's most notable characters, who became very annoyed when Sir Claud Huntbath called him Mr. MacDonald:

"It is the custom in my country to address me as Ben Nevis," the Chieftain repeated, the amaranth of his eagle's beak by now showing signs of deepening even to the blue-black of the raven's wing.

The Permanent Secretary groped back into the shadowland of his childhood when he had read the novels of Sir Walter Scott. . . . He must try to forget that Ben Nevis was the highest mountain in the British Isles and accept it as the name of a tall gentleman with hair like his pet Airedale. . . . [4]

Oliver Huffam visits Ben Nevis's ancestral home, Glenbogle Castle, which has a great hall hung with Lochaber axes, muskets, stags' heads, and the portraits of kilted chieftains. No sooner is Huffam seated for dinner than "the doors of the dining-hall were flung open to admit two pipers in full blast, who proceeded to march round and round the table, making what Huffam thought was a most unreasonable noise." Mackenzie brings in the full Scottish Highland paraphernalia of craggy and draughty castles, kilted chieftains and suspicious gamekeepers, bagpipe laments, legends of ancient massacres and modern sea serpents, and complaints about London's indifference to the fate of the Highlands and the local authority's indifference to the condition of the roads. It is hard for an outsider to judge how realistically he has portrayed a man like Ben Nevis, but there is testimony to his accuracy in the fact that not one but several Highland ladies accused him of using their husbands as models for the laird of Glenbogle.[5]

I *The Monarch of the Glen*

The Monarch of the Glen (1941), the first of the novels set mainly or entirely in Scotland, is one of the best. Mackenzie began it while under the strain of writing a section of a major serious novel, *The*

Four Winds of Love; for, as so often, he took refuge in writing a comic book. Published in 1941, it was a victim of wartime conditions: "Unfortunately only 3000 of the 7000 copies subscribed could be supplied because the Post Office demanded the paper for a telephone directory."[6] This novel is especially interesting for the range of attitudes to Scottish matters which it reveals and for the light it throws on Mackenzie's comic methods.

In *The Red Tapeworm,* we observed the contrast between a colorful Scots laird and two colorless English bureaucrats. Mackenzie generally relies on such strong and striking contrasts. In *The Monarch of the Glen,* Ben Nevis is set against Sydney Prew, secretary of the National Union of Hikers, "a dark desiccated little man"; the Acting President of the same organization, Percy Buckham, one of the live wires of the advertising world, the "he-man with the heart of a boy"; and the President, Lord Buntingdon of Ouse Hall, a slow-moving man with a melon-shaped head. Not all of the contrasts are with unsympathetic people; Carrie Royde, whose great-great-grandfather was dispossessed by an ancestor of Ben Nevis's, comes to her ancestral homeland from the United States and sees everything through a romantic glow. Her husband Chester is used more specifically for comic incongruity — when he is dressed for the moors, he looks "like a full-page advertisement in the pages of *Esquire* or *Vanity Fair* designed to haunt, to startle and waylay the most casual reader"; and he even exceeds this dress when he turns up at Glenbogle's Gathering in a flame-colored kilt.

These strong contrasts give Mackenzie a whole range of comic possibilities. For example, he can expose Chester Royde to an utterly inhuman experience for a New York financier — a deer stalk which involves two miles of crawling and submersion under one of the biggest rainstorms since the Deluge, only to find that the stag has disappeared. Or the romantic approach of the Roydes to the Highlands can be set against the natives' shrewd practicality — as when Chester says, "I aim to buy a place up here," and Ben Nevis's best friend perks up his ears: "Kilwhillie's faded eyes were lighted up with that strange light which never was on sea or land, but is only to be seen in the eyes of a landed proprietor in the Highlands who hopes he has found a buyer for an overtaxed forest of twelve heads and a shooting-lodge that looks like a bunch of tarnished pepper-pots."[7]

As this quotation shows, Mackenzie can take a realistic view of the Scottish scene. The many caves in which Bonnie Prince Charlie is reputed to have hidden, the less melodious of noises on the bagpipe, the ancient feuds and animosities — many such features of Highland life are looked at with an amused eye. In addition, a note of objectivity is introduced through the viewpoint of a sensible sassenach — Ben Nevis's English wife: "She would have liked to strip from the walls their frieze of substantial Victorian wallpaper depicting stags in every attitude a stag can put itself into. . . . There were moments when the steel-engravings of MacDonalds overwhelming Macintoshes in battle palled upon her. . . . " But the divisions and antipathies among the Scots themselves are also sources of comedy. For example, we cite Ben Nevis's reaction when he is asked what he thinks of Scottish Nationalists:

> The tints of the dying dolphin at their most vivid and varied would have seemed drab compared with the tints that displayed themselves upon the countenance of the Chieftain when he heard this question. The hats of cardinals, the shirts of Garibaldi's legionaries, the flags of the world revolution, the ribbons of O. B. E. s, [the Order of the British Empire], the plumes of flamingoes, the tails of redstarts, the breasts of robins, the skies that warn or delight shepherds according to the time, the tunics of grenadiers and the tape of the Civil Service mingled and melted, flamed and faltered, and flamed again in his cheeks.[8]

Needless to say, Mackenzie produces some Scottish Nationalists who have equally strong views about decadent landed proprietors who are chiefly interested in shooting and in stalking game. Ben Nevis plans to hunt them down and throw them into the nearest loch, and they plan to kidnap him as a symbolic gesture.

Ultimately, however, Ben Nevis and the Nationalists are brought into reluctant collaboration; the main conflict lies elsewhere. At the beginning of the novel, a painter is busy putting up "No Camping" signs since Glenbogle is becoming infested with hikers. On that day of supreme importance, the twelfth of August — the opening of the grouse-shooting season — the first major engagement takes place. Ben Nevis's hopes of a record bag are shattered when hardly a bird is seen on the moor of Drumcockie; trespassers have apparently scared them away. When the irate chieftain learns where these interlopers are camping, he quickly forms his party in martial array and takes the hikers by surprise. He shakes Mr. Prew as a conscientious housemaid shakes a mat; he fires both barrels of his gun into a radio from which a crooner is blaring forth; and he marches his afternoon's bag of sixteen hikers off to his castle where he shuts the male miscreants in the dungeon under the Raven's Tower and the females in the one under the North Tower.

The subsequent action, as Chester Royde's sister Myrtle says, " 'makes Chicago seem kind of slow and sleepy.' " Mrs. MacDonald releases the women prisoners and placates them with a meal, but the eight male hikers are uncompromising in their hostility and leave only after threatening the worst reprisals. Ben Nevis has the satisfaction of harrying them all the way down the glen with a motorized column consisting of a truck, his pre-1914 Daimler, and two small cars; he returns from the operation in boisterous good humor. But the hikers call a special meeting in Astrovegetarian Hall in London, and there, after they have harrowed an audience with tales of the indignities they suffered, Percy Buckham gets the national organization to join in a "tremendous manifestation of Youth, Freedom and Democracy against the forces of Reaction and Fascism." On the day of the Glenbogle Gathering, Ben Nevis smiles on all comers, even a busload of hikers — suspecting nothing. But at the end of the day, Chester Royde can't be found; the hikers have kidnapped him.

A letter from the National Union of Hikers informs Ben Nevis that "when a great democratic institution decides to take offensive action it can act with greater vigour, effect, speed and ruthlessness than any dictator." For a time, this statement seems entirely true; the hikers executed the capture of Chester with considerable skill; and when Ben Nevis takes a party out to stalk them, this whole group is ambushed, tied up, and put in a cave once reputedly used as a refuge by Prince Charles Edward. Naturally they are rescued — but by the despised Scottish Nationalists. Furthermore, shortly before this rescue they have listened with amazement to Percy Buckham say, "I want to give you the pleasure, Mr. MacDonald, of seeing with your own eyes my forces march into Glenbogle Castle, pull down that flag of yours with half the Zoo on it, and hoist the crossed staffs of the N. U. H. [National Union of Hikers]". Restored to his seat, Ben Nevis prepares for assault; he thinks of defending his towers and ramparts with boiling water — "I'd like to use boiling oil, but I doubt if we've got enough oil to boil" — but settles for pails of soapy water, which are used with very good effect. The issue hangs in the balance, however, until Ben Nevis hears pipers playing a tune more hateful to him than even "The Hiker's Song": to the strains of "The Campbells Are Coming," "the kilted members of the Scottish Brotherhood of Action, like a tartan catalogue come to life," crack into the courtyard and rout the hikers. Ben Nevis remains monarch in his glen, and next year the grouse will be better than ever.

The plot line is clearly intended to produce the broad comic contrasts we have noticed and as much rip-roaring, farcical action as possible. The setting is sufficiently remote from our everyday experience for the hurling of hikers into dungeons not to appear too audacious a stroke on the author's part; it is Ben Nevis's modern-day equivalent of his ancestors' ruthlessness. Describing his hero's lineage, Mackenzie parodies the bloodthirsty legends associated with every Scottish clan. In the year 1546, so Carrie Royde reads in *Happy Days Among the Heather,* a party of marauding Macintoshes were surprised and killed by the MacDonalds of Ben Nevis; some years later the Macintoshes baked thirty-two old and infirm MacDonalds in an oven; and for this Hector the ninth of Ben Nevis burned forty-five Macintoshes in a church one Sunday morning while his piper improvised a tune and played it to drown their shrieks.[9] Mackenzie can describe with both affection and amusement his eccentric Highlanders and their history.

II *War in the Western Isles*

Discussing *The Monarch* and its successors, Leo Robertson writes, "His characters once created seem to live lives of their own, carrying them beyond the limits of any tale in which they figure. . . . in writing about these well-loved Highlanders of his Compton Mackenzie has opened a door leading into a realm of his own where he has friends of every sort from laird to crofter, to whom it is our privilege to be introduced when he chooses to write about them."[10] This statement is even more true, however, of characters from the Hebrides than of mainlanders like Ben Nevis. "Last night we listened to the 2nd part of your 'Keep the Home Guard Turning' on the wireless and what a laugh!" Duncan Sinclair writes Mackenzie from Barra. "Everyone could figure some of the prototypes."[11]

When the foundation stone of Mackenzie's house on Barra was laid on the day commemorating the Silver Jubilee of King George V in 1935, Father John Macmillan delivered a speech of welcome in which he said, "You came to assimilate our life. . . . A golden circle of nobleness and character used to surround Eilean na h'Oige [the island of Youth]. That circle, although not broken and shattered altogether, suffered the coming of a world whose ways are artificial and insincere. It is up to us, with your co-operation and help, to repair the damage done to that golden circle."[12] On the evidence of his memoirs and novels, Mackenzie was seemingly admitted into a golden circle of affection and good humor which, as Robertson says, he lets his readers glimpse from time to time.

Barra lies near the two Uists, North and South, which Mackenzie converts into Great and Little Todday in his novels. The former is the home of the MacRuries and Protestant; the latter, that of the Macroons and Catholic; and rivalry has existed between the two families from time immemorial. The dominant figure on Great Todday is the keeper of the Hotel Snorvig, Roderick MacRurie: " . . . in spite of his ruthless business methods, his tall tales, his ferocious whisky, and it was believed his enormous wealth, Great Todday was proud of Roderick MacRurie. . . . The people of Great Todday felt that Ruaridh Mór came as near to the giant pirate they acknowledged as their original patriarch as any Great Toddy man had come since the immense form of the redoubtable Ruaridh Ruadh himself vanished from the eyes of men." Perhaps the second most respected figure is the doctor, Dr. Maclaren, a "jovial, hard-drinking and thoroughly competent" medical man.

But a wide range of personalities populate the island, from these two colorful figures all the way down to the ferocious Mrs. Campbell, who locks her son the schoolteacher in his bedroom so that he won't be able to take part in a Home Guard exercise on the Sabbath. Joseph Macroon, postmaster and leading merchant of Little Todday, is Roderick MacRurie's opposite number; he is "a small sharp-featured man with a trim grey moustache, quick in his movements, who always wore a knitted red cap such as trolls wear in illustrated fairy tales." But the commanding personality on the island is the portly Father James Macalister, who is shrewdly aware of the character and capabilities of everyone on his island, a lover of whisky and lobsters who is always prepared to view the comic side of things. Again there is a whole gallery of eccentric personalities on the island, including, for example, "a man with tumbled fair hair, a glowing countenance, and eyes as blue as the wing of a kingfisher," Duncan Macroon, who sits with a bottle of whisky on Tràig Swish and declaims Gaelic poetry to the flowing tide, but also proves to be a military tactician of great skill.

The society Mackenzie describes is both simple and complex. It has its superstitions; when Duncan Macroon leads twenty men wearing respirators in a mock attack on Great Todday, the children run screaming from what they think are *bòcain* or ghosts; and, when Duncan himself talks about receiving poetic inspiration from a good kind fairy lady who has been washing his clothes all winter, we are not certain whether he is telling a tall tale or not. When a native of the Toddays is talking to an outsider, however, we may be pretty sure that he will amuse himself by a pretense either of sympathy or of ignorance. When two self-important naval officers are trying to impress upon the police constable, Mr. Macrae, that because Great Todday and Little Todday are in separate Protected Areas no travelers may cross the two miles between them without a permit, he is more than a match for them:

"And what about myself?" Macrae asked. "Do I give myself a permit to visit Little Todday? And *vice versa* of course."

"I sent you full instructions about the procedure to be adopted," said Captain Quiblick reproachfully.

"So did I," said Captain Lomax-Smith.

"So did the Chief Constable," Macrae added, beaming. "And I've had a lot of instructions about the procedure to adopt with German submarines who come to either of the two islands without a permit."

"Well, I don't know anything about German submarines . . . ," Captain Quiblick began.

"Nor do I," said Macrae.

"They don't come under Security Intelligence."

"What a pity," said Macrae sympathetically. "I believe you'd make a good job with them, sir."

Captain Quiblick darted the penetrating glance of a Security Intelligence Officer at the constable, but Macrae's eyes were innocent of sarcasm.[13]

The major target for mockery in *Keep the Home Guard Turning* (1943), however, is a resident, if not a native, of Great Todday. Five years before World War II began, a London chartered accountant named Paul Waggett responded to the romantic notion of becoming a landed proprietor by buying the tumbledown house of the last of the MacRurie chieftains, together with the lease of the shooting and fishing rights for the two islands. Ever since, he has been posing before visitors as the laird of the Toddays, and vainly trying to keep the islanders from catching his fish and shooting his grouse. When the Local Defence Volunteers (soon to become the Home Guard) are organized, Ben Nevis's friend Colonel Lindsey-Wolseley asks Waggett to raise a company from the Toddays. Waggett gets a very good response, not because of his own popularity but because the uncrowned king of Great Todday, Roderick MacRurie, and the unmitred bishop of Little Todday, Father Macalister, support him. He is a greedy hypocrite, meticulous in enforcing the regulations he is supposed to administer, but not above hoarding anything which is on ration or may possibly go on ration. What a pity, he thinks, that he is too old to serve in the active forces since he always knows what the Germans are going to do next. To his second in command, John

Beaton, a burly school headmaster, he explains the need for road-blocks on the islands, "as nonchalantly as if enemy tanks were a feature of the sporting amenities of Todday." There comes a day, consequently, when, after Doctor Maclaren has superintended the birth of a set of twins and is heading homeward with the thought of supper and a stiff whisky in his mind, he finds the road blocked by a thicket of barbed wire which two of his own patients refuse to allow him through, and tries another road only to run into another thicket of barbed wire separating him from his whisky. He finds the appropriate judgment for the man in charge of the obstructions: "Mr. Waggett, as an emetic you'd make a bottle of ipecacuanha as mild as a glass of sherry."

The events of this novel are set against the "sombre tale of French catastrophe." The day when Captain Waggett got the telegram with the single word "Balloon" — the code word to say that the invasion had started, the day when Alan Macdonald of Little Todday mistook a barrel of herrings for the Germans and fired a shot which produced an outbreak of firing all around the island — was the day when in actuality rumors of invasion ran all up and down the west coast of Britain. The farcical incidents described in the novel are mock-heroic in nature, but it took a certain amount of heroism for Captain Waggett to leave his home and his wife and make a circuit of his island to ensure that, if the Germans did land, there would be a few graybeards of the Home Guard ready to meet them.

The serious, even sombre background to the events is always present, therefore; yet in the foreground is a series of military adventures which is absolutely hilarious. On the day Hitler invades Russia, Ben Nevis invades the Toddays at the head of his company of Home Guardsmen — ostensibly in a practice landing, actually in search of the left boot of a pair which has been allotted to his company but has somehow been separated. There is a great deal of satire on expected topics, such as the outfitting of the volunteers with clothes in the standard sizes of too large or too small, or the equipping them with rifles of one caliber and ammunition of another. There is a good deal of fun also with military terminology and cant phrases, as when Brigadier Beamish says that the people at the top are tremendously keen on "suspicious alertness" and exhorts the men of the Toddays to be in a permanent condition of "suspicious alertness." But, as this last example shows, the satire moves beyond the officiousness of the wooden-headed Waggett to the officiousness of bureaucrats everywhere.

And best of all is the placing of Little Todday in Protected Area 13 and Great Todday in Protected Area 14, so that the crossing of the channel between them is forbidden, except by a special permit which must be applied for several weeks in advance. The novel is the epic story of how the two Toddays manage to survive, not the war, but the bureaucracy to which the war gives such a golden opportunity. The last paragraph puts the situation in perspective for us:

G Company are still turning. They have just learnt to substitute tempo for suspicious alertness and to speak of being checked instead of being held up. . . . . Their weapons have been dealt and re-dealt as often as a pack of cards at progressive whist. Their boots are getting worn out, but they are still proud of them, and it is as well they are, for they are not likely to get any more for a long while. And since the two islands are still in two different protected areas, the people of Great Britain can feel secure. Hitler is not likely to land on either island without a permit, and if he does, the pikes are waiting for him.

III   *Scotch on the Rocks*

The best-known of the Scottish novels is more specifically an account of wartime deprivation and its temporary alleviation. The story had a basis in fact: early in 1941, the *S. S. Politician* took the wrong direction on her way out of the Minch to the Atlantic and struck a rock off the island of Eriskay, which is close to Barra. In *Scotch on the Rocks: The True Story of the 'Whisky Galore' Ship,* Arthur Swinson has done an intriguing investigation of the accident. He is not able to solve the problem of why it occurred; the ship was miles off course for no apparent reason. Perhaps the people of the Outer Hebrides had a right to believe that it was because of a benign act of Providence, as Mackenzie comments in *My Life and Times —* and Swinson gives a translation of a very amusing Gaelic ballad on the theme: "So here's a health to the Captain bold/ Of the good ship *Politician!*/ And here's to the rock she struck that night,/ A-sailing on her mission!" In a foreword to Swinson's book, Mackenzie compliments the latter on his dogged pursuit of the facts, but he asks one question which the book does not answer: why were twenty thousand cases of Scotch whisky shipped from Liverpool aboard the *Politician* and how did they get there? He himself provides a possible reply:

I have been told that the Secretary of State for Scotland, the Right Honourable Thomas Johnston, after a lot of whisky was lost by enemy action in Glasgow and in Leith, decided that no more of the precious liquid should be wasted by German bombs and gave orders for all the whisky available to be immediately evacuated. At a Highland gathering . . . after that great Scottish Secretary had been talking about hydroelectricity I told the audience that much as I admired his achievements over water I was even more grateful for his prompt action over whisky, thanks to which so many of his countrymen were able to enjoy, free of duty, their native spirit in the land that produced it.

And I take this opportunity of declaring that the destruction of so much of that whisky by the Customs and Excise adds one more example to the long and dreary record of bureaucratic hebetude. Cherishing as I do a deep regard and affection for those men and women of the West with whom I lived so happily for many years I am glad to be assured by Mr. Swinson that a third of that cargo was salvaged by those who had a moral right to it whatever the law might say.[14]

As Swinson shows, it was bad enough for the excisemen to obstruct the hazardous business of fishing for the whisky cases in the oily hold of the ship, and bad enough again for them to search for the whisky and destroy it when they found it, but the thing for which they could never be forgiven was the dynamiting of the ship when there were still thousands of cases aboard her.

Discussing the success of the novel and of the film made from it (released under the title *Tight Little Island* in the United States), Mackenzie told Swinson that "Its fascination must be that it is really a modern fairy story — someone looking for treasure and finding it." Swinson puts it differently: "To me, its great charm is that it does what so few novels do in English literature, that is reflect the life of a whole community, ignoring completely any artificial barriers of class or money. It also has the earthy, healthy tang of a folk novel. Many people, I believe, consider it contains the only successful attempt to capture the flavour of the Gaelic speech of the Islanders, and translate it into English. For this novel alone, not to mention the film, I shall always be grateful to the *Politician,* and of course to Sir Compton who was, most remarkably, living in the right place at the right time."[15]

Mackenzie establishes first in the book the terrible nature of the drought that has afflicted the Toddays. Sergeant-major Odd, who appeared in *Keep the Home Guard Turning,* comes back to the islands after eighteen months' absence and is struck by the pervading gloom. A quotation from Hector Hamish Mackay's travel book *Faerie Lands Forlorn* now takes on an ironic character: "In our host's snuggery the glasses reflect with opalescent gleams the flicker

of a welcome fire of peats, and as we raise the *uisge beatha* [water of life] to our lips . . . we feel that we are indeed privileged visitors. . . . "
"Tempora mutantur," Mackenzie continues. "This evening an almost silent group of elderly or old or very old men sat on the wooden benches round the bar and eyed the glasses of beer on the tables in front of them without relish. Beer does not taste like itself unless it is chasing a dram of neat whisky down the gullet, preferably two drams."[16]

That very night, Roderick MacRurie is forced to tell Captain Alec MacPhee, the patriarch of Snorvig who is now in his ninetieth year, that the two pints of beer he has already had are all he will be allowed; and the old man goes home to die of the shock. Only Paul Waggett still has some whisky left; having denied it to the minister's wife, who wants some for her husband's cold, he measures out a careful dram to ward off germs from himself and with a superior smile talks about improvidence as the besetting sin of the islands. As to the Sergeant-major, the great drought makes it impossible for him to make Joseph Macroon fix a date for his marriage to Joseph's daughter Peggy; what is the use of thinking of a wedding, when there is no whisky to be had? Even Father Macalister describes himself as like a wireless set with no battery: "Look at me now. Here's an old friend back from barbarous places like Africa and Devonshire, and I haven't a sensation to offer him, not so much as a wee snifter."

Conditions get worse before they get better; and, in the eighth chapter, entitled "The Drought," Dr. Maclaren describes the catastrophic conditions in a long passage naming those he is sorry for (including Father James and himself "because both of us really require fortifying"), especially "old Hector MacRurie who has made up his mind that he will shortly have to face his Maker without a dram inside him to sustain him through the ordeal." The Saturday-night gathering at Roderick's bar has to eke out half a pint of beer per head until closing time; they "passed out into the clammy darkness of the fog that night like ghosts from a happier age." Just at this point, the *S. S. Cabinet Minister* runs onto a black reef just off Little Todday; and the two Clydesiders who come ashore in the captain's cutter shake the imperturbability of the first islanders they meet by telling them that the ship is carrying fifty thousand cases of whisky.

Whisky Galore is a very merry book. Mackenzie places the *Cabinet Minister* in a much more convenient location for the surreptitious removal of her cargo than was the case with the *Politician,* and the hazards of the enterprise, as well as the opposition of the ex-cisemen, are minimized. The romantic aspect of the affair which Mackenzie commented on to Swinson is strongly in his mind in the novel: "Many romantic pages have been written about the sunken Spanish galleon in the bay of Tobermory. That 4000-ton steamship on the rocks off Little Todday provided more practical romance in three and a half hours than the Tobermory galleon has provided in three and a half centuries. Doubloons, ducats, and ducatoons, moidores, pieces of eight, sequins, guineas, rose and angel nobles, what are these to vaunt above the liquid gold carried by the *Cabinet Minister?"* And he calls the role of both famous and obscure brands of Scotch included in the collection: Highland Gold and Highland Heart, Tartan Gold and Tartan Perfection, and fifty more. "There were spherical bottles and dimpled bottles and square bottles and oblong bottles and flagon-shaped bottles and high-waisted bottles and ordinary bottles," he concludes, "and the glass of every bottle was stamped with a notice which made it clear that whisky like this was intended to be drunk in the United States of America and not by the natives of the land where it was distilled, matured and blended."[17]

This providential outpouring of liquid gold enables Sergeant-major Odd and Peggy Macroon to have as fine a *Rèiteach,* or betrothal party, as has been seen on Little Todday for many a year. As a result George Campbell the schoolmaster, "thanks to two drams of Pipe Major, two drams of Fingal's Cave and three fingers of Annie Laurie," possesses the courage to confront the old harridan his mother; to tell her that, in future, she will do what he says or he will turn her out of the house; and to announce that he is going to marry Catriona Macleod in a month's time. The only threat to the islanders' enjoyment of the Minnie (as the whisky gets called) is that pompous Waggett would like to have his Home Guard made respon-sible for the security of the cargo and, failing in that, does his best to stir up the authorities. Even these officials are unusually benevolent; Major Quiblick, the Security Officer, and Tom Ferguson, the Ex-ciseman, come to investigate, after they have received complaints about the market in spirits on the Toddays, but they merely let themselves be seen making inquiries, sail around the wreck, and return to their home base with two cases of whisky for themselves. The only major catastrophe in the latter part of the novel occurs because Peggy and Kate Macroon become frightened of prison when Quiblick and Ferguson appear and empty two hundred and sixteen bottles onto the floor of their father's shed.

Swinson has reason to stress that *Whisky Galore* presents the life of a whole community from the highest to the lowest social levels. Indeed, the novel is a kind of comic prose epic that deals with a great crisis in the life of a people, its overcoming, and the rejoicing in consequence — as it occurs particularly in two formal celebrations, the already-mentioned betrothal and the wedding of the Sergeant-major and Peggy which concludes the story. Because of the overriding comic vision, the possible threats are minimized, banished, or rendered contemptible.

Bureaucracy sends a Lieutenant Boggust, posing as a traveler in tweed named Mr. Brown, who comes to investigate Waggett's complaint to Quiblick that a wave of defeatism is sweeping the Toddays. A thin young man with a "neo-Caroline moustache" and "plus-fours of the barrage balloon type," he gets short shrift from most of the people he tries to interview; and he has to endure a Sunday on Protestant Great Todday, where even a game of cribbage would be regarded as a wild violation of the Sabbath, where a shocked rejection greets his request for some whisky, and where his dinner consists of some cold mutton so tough and desiccated that he wonders whether it is the heel or the sole. The only people in the islands who thrive on the discomfort of their neighbors, Waggett and Mrs. Campbell, also get the treatment they deserve — she is finally put in her place by her son; and he is treated by Quiblick, Ferguson, and Constable Macrae as "a man who thinks he's General Montgomery and isn't him at all." Even the outsiders who come into the story are congenial, especially Sergeant-major Odd, who of course has a special reason for identifying himself with the community's point of view, and his remarkable mother, a delightfully garrulous old woman who comes to the wedding at the end of the book. Mackenzie has subdued his own indignation at bureaucratic stupidity and turned the wreck of the good ship *Politician* into an entirely pleasant memory — the way it will chiefly live in the minds of the islanders.

IV   *Other Scottish Novels*

Hunting the Fairies (1949) starts with an unsentimental view of a Highland residence: "The Highlands are not rich in domestic architecture. The really beautiful old houses can easily be enumerated on ten fingers. Kilwhillie House is not one of them. It is an ancient grim grey square edifice. . . . " Then follows an unsentimental view of the laird himself: "A small man with a head of the button type and a pair of long thin dark drooping moustaches. . . , he was wearing a faded kilt. . . , a leather sporran limp with age, and a doublet of cigar-brown Harris tweed." Against this dour neighbor of Ben Nevis are set two formidable American women, rivals for the presidency of the Ossianic Society of Boston, who engage in a hilarious competition for specimens of Gaelic folklore. But almost the whole spectrum of possible attitudes to the Scottish past is brought into the novel, and Mackenzie exploits their comic possibilities very adroitly.

In *The Rival Monster* (1952) Mackenzie uses both his mainland and island groups of characters: a strange creature takes up residence in a cave on Poppay in which Joseph Macroon has some of his Scotch whisky hidden, and Ben Nevis and his entourage go to hunt the monster out of its lair and find out whether it is a genuine rival for the Loch Ness sea serpent. It is a complicated tale with a large cast of characters, which Mackenzie handles well; the suspense is kept to the very end — the rival monster is a walrus.

Ben Nevis Goes East (1954) is noteworthy only for showing how easily Mackenzie could have relapsed into the use of a formula in his Scottish novels. Having been in India himself, Mackenzie seizes on the humorous possibilities of putting Ben Nevis into this entirely incongruous setting; and he produces humor of a completely predictable kind, involving, for example, the inevitable tiger hunt. The epilogue shows the contrast operating in another direction: the chieftain returns home, demands gimlets instead of Scotch whisky, and serves his neighbors a curry so hot they can't eat it.

Rockets Galore (1957) has a much more serious theme; it is no mere mechanical sequel to *Whisky Galore* but a humorous treatment of another controversy in which Mackenzie was involved. On July 27, 1955, the British government announced that a range would be established on South Uist in the Hebrides for training forces in the use of guided missiles. The announcement benignly stated that the range would be relatively small and would benefit the islanders in many ways. The protests inundating Scots papers for weeks suggested what kind of valuation could be put on these promises; there was also a very good letter in the *Times,* temperate in tone, signed by nine prominent people, including Mackenzie, which pointed out that the population of South Uist was fully employed and that the kind of scheme which would benefit a depressed area was not needed there. About a month later, Air Marshal J. C. Slessor suggested that the opponents of the scheme should not weaken their case by behaving as though the Air Ministry were a lot of soulless vandals and that the authorities on the other hand should do their utmost to meet the very real objections. He added that he knew only too well that, whenever the Air Ministry wanted to establish a range, the site selected turns out to be the only habitat of some rare bird. To this Peter Scott, the naturalist, replied that South Uist was indeed the home of the only remaining large colony of grey lag geese![18] This statement gave Mackenzie the humorous twist he needed, when, with the passage of time, he calmed down sufficiently to write a novel on the subject. The Air Force *did* get its rocket range — but it was still causing controversy fourteen years later.

Father James Macalister, the doughty leader of the islands' defense against rockets in Mackenzie's novel, makes it clear that he is trying to defend a culture against "the damnable juggernaut they call progress." The point is made when he talks to an Irish girl named Jane Kinsella, who wants to learn to sing in opera. He tells her, "if you go to Milan and get taught to sing in the Italian style you'll be no more use for singing as you do now, and that would be a pity." Her songs are a pure delight because she sings them as simply and naturally as a thrush at dawn. He asks Hugh MacInnes whether he has heard of the lost Atlantis; receiving a vaguely affirmative response, he says, "Well, there's still a little bit of it left in the Islands, but it won't last very long the way the world is going, and it is our duty to preserve it as long as we can. . . . "[19] On such a basis he fights the proposed rocket range. When an exploratory mission of armed forces bigwigs and a rocket expert named Dr. Hamburger come to visit him, he denies people hospitality for the first time in his life: "Not even a dram did I offer them."

Not all the islanders are opposed to the project, as Mrs. Odd explains: "Oh, I don't doubt but what you'll get quite a few people on Great Todday to tell you that everything in the garden's lovely. I'll lay every lorry-driver in the island sees himself as Lord Nuffield the Second with the money coming to him. And I lay all the girls are rocking and rolling with joy already to think of American G. I.'s handing out nylons and chewing-gum and cigarettes."[20] But the ineptitude of the bureaucrats quickly consolidates the opposition — especially when they blow up the harbor of Kiltod (to build a new pier) on a Sunday morning and when they secure eviction orders against twenty-two crofters. The authorities do not know how to get rid of the turbulent priest who is standing in their way — they do not even know what to call him — and they waver between oily statements that they intend no harm to the civilian population and orders to evacuate the civilian population of the islands entirely on grounds of national security. Moreover, they are sometimes inclined to confuse Gaelic with Russian.

Mackenzie no doubt exaggerates ministerial and military ignorance; at the same time, he goes very far towards establishing his major criticism: that the officials in London do not know the people they are dealing with. A brief episode, which might be called "The Colonel, the Marshal, and the Biffer," typifies their attitude and the reaction of the islanders to them. "You're even further from civilization here than they are in Balmuir," the Colonel observes to the boatman ferrying the exploratory mission from Great to Little Todday. The Biffer asks whether civilization is one of those new housing estates they have; and, when the Colonel patiently explains that civilization is not a place, the Biffer answers, "I know what civilization is here in the Islands. But I never heard you had that kind of civilization down in England."

The Air Chief Marshal then asks, in a tone of indulgent condescension, "So you don't think we're civilized down in London?" "Och, it's not your fault," says the Biffer. "You're all too busy getting on in the world. You don't have any time for meditation." "I'm afraid we shouldn't get very far in this world if we all went in for too much meditation," the Marshall replies. "No, I believe you wouldn't," the Biffer agrees. "But you might get a great deal further in the next world."[21] The point Mackenzie makes so effectively is that the people in authority are half-educated men who treat the islanders as though they were aborigines, whereas the Macroons and MacRuries have their own kind of wisdom which needs to be respected.

Mackenzie perhaps goes too far in making the strategic considerations behind the missile range equally simple-minded; from his point of view, the question reduces itself to such commonplaces as that the Russians are not going to attack the West and that, if they did, such rockets as are proposed for British defense would not do any good anyway. He also goes too far in some of the obstructive measures with which he expects us to sympathize, as when a missile called a Thunderbuzzard lands on Little Todday by mistake and the inhabitants hack it to pieces. But he is not wildly in error in the measure which he devises to produce a happier ending for his novel than the controversy had in actuality. After the evacuation of Little Todday has been ordered, the situation seems hopeless until Hugh MacInnes gets his great idea: he captures some gulls and paints them pink. He brings an ornithologist friend, Martin Leslie, to see them; and Martin becomes wildly excited though he suffers tortures because he cannot land on the rocky island of Pillay and examine their nests, their eggs, and their young (Hugh has got his job done just before the fine weather breaks). With suitable irony, Mackenzie describes the campaign which ensues — the television broadcasts, the letters to the papers, the demonstrations in Trafalgar Square — and the government's surrender over birds when it had been adamant over people. Coming the way it does, the decision to back down is only another instance of distorted or perverted values: the destruction of the way of life of a thousand people is viewed with complacency, but a threat to the habitat of a rare bird is soon stopped.

The foregoing outline of the argument of *Rockets Galore* gives very little idea of its humor; its superb comic invention almost puts it in the class of *Whisky Galore*. This creativity applies particularly to the imaginative schemes which the islanders concoct to discomfit their oppressors. The giants in office are really pygmies, and it is not hard for the Macroons and MacRuries to outwit them; still they are malicious pygmies who have powers entirely disproportionate to their wisdom. In this frank caricature of Whitehall bureaucrats and gold-braided officers, Mackenzie is demonstrably unfair; but he is not so unfair as to make us sympathetic towards them. His case is so well argued that it is completely convincing. If the people of the Hebrides live an anomalous life as compared to most other residents of Great Britain, their sturdy individualism, strong principles, and keen enjoyment of life make us feel that the more such anomalies the better.

CHAPTER 9

Memoirs of a Prodigal Romantic

I *War Memoirs*

IF Mackenzie's amazing memory served him well in fiction, it was bound to serve him equally well for reminiscences, especially because he had a range of experiences considerably beyond that of the average novelist. He wrote two main series of memoirs: the first deals with his wartime experiences; the second, with the whole span of his life. The four volumes of war memories began appearing in 1929; but, because of the withdrawal of *Greek Memories* (1932) and Mackenzie's prosecution for publishing it, the last was not published until 1940. In the preface to *Gallipoli Memories,* (1929), he explains that ever since the war he had been meditating a war novel: "Indeed I have long had an immense affair in seven volumes mapped out; but I have finally come to the conclusion that my experiences in Athens and the Cyclades will make a better novel if related as fact. I cannot imagine more richly tragical, comical, and farcical characters than I actually met."[1] His stated object was "to recapture the spirit in which I passed through a memorable experience."

An additional object in the volumes dealing with Greece was obviously to set the record straight: "This first volume adds nothing of the least historical value to the literature of the war, though in succeeding volumes I hope to shed some light on the situation in Greece during 1916 and 1917, which, obscure enough in any case, has been still further obscured by a mass of partisan writing on both sides." He was still a doughty partisan of Venizelos, the Greek premier. But even in the first volume he had a case to argue, the case of an Easterner versus a Westerner — one who believed that the war could have been won much earlier if the Dardanelles campaign had been pushed with vigor. His wife wrote, "Monty succumbed to

[123]

sciatica after finishing the first part of his Gallipoli reminiscences. It's not surprising; his whole heart and soul were in it and I've never seen him so passionately engrossed since *Sinister Street.*"[2] It is no wonder that the book received warm praise from General Sir Ian Hamilton, the Allied Commander in the Gallipoli Campaign.

Mackenzie tells the story of his own involvement in the war most engagingly. He describes how crestfallen he was when a soldier friend at the War Office told him he was not wanted: "Go back to your work. You'll be doing more good by keeping us cheerful with your novels. We really do not want married subalterns of thirty-one."[3] Reflecting the mood of the times, he evidently tried to join the forces both because he wanted to serve his country and because he did not want to miss the experience of being in action. When Orlo Williams wrote to tell him that he had secured him a job with General Hamilton, he concluded his letter by saying, "The General Staff are a charming set of people, and the possibilities of this show are romantic to a degree."[4]

The Eastern Mediterranean contained many a legendary beauty spot which would appeal to Mackenzie's temperament:

> On Friday, the twenty-fifth of June, I set out early in the morning for that island dearly loved by Apollo. . . . I firmly believe that when a philonese who has had a wide practical experience of islands steps ashore on a fresh strand he knows immediately whether or not he has fed on honey-dew. . . . That is always the problem of the new island. Is it a world within a world within infinity, or but the empty shell of a perfect world? Land upon Capri, upon Iona, upon Samos, upon Tenedos, upon my own Shiant Islands, and you are aware of completeness. . . .[5]

The Aegean offered innumerable islands for a connoisseur to savor, and Mackenzie immensely enjoyed them. But how about the war which, after all, was his excuse for traveling? Could he view it romantically too? His description of some of the fighting men reveals that he could:

> Much has been written about the splendid appearance of those Australian troops; but a splendid appearance seems to introduce somehow an atmosphere of the parade-ground. Such litheness and powerful grace did not want the parade ground; that was to take it from the jungle to the circus. Their beauty, for it really was heroic, should have been celebrated in hexameters not headlines. As a child I used to pore for hours over those illustrations of Flaxman for Homer and Virgil which simulated the effect of

ancient pottery. There was not one of those glorious young men I saw that day who might not himself have been Ajax or Diomed, Hector or Achilles.[6]

Mackenzie was in a curiously detached and objective position: "of 1915 I am writing as the mere observer and from an angle completely unvexed by responsibility," "I should be at Gallipoli a mere butterfly in a graveyard." He lost a bit of that detachment when he came under fire: "Small shells kept dropping all round me, and it seemed inevitable that I should be hit presently. There is no doubt that the sensation of being shelled when alone is most infernally unpleasant. . . . I began to worry about the proofs of *Guy and Pauline,* thinking to myself that the printer's reader would be sure to change 'tralucent' to 'translucent' and that Secker in the depression caused by the news of my death would never remember how much importance I attached to getting rid of that unnecessary sibilant."[7]

He is very apologetic about an encouraging report about the low state of Turkish morale which he composed under orders — "And God forgive me, this is what I wrote" — though he says that at the time he sincerely hoped that the twaddle he set down was not far from the truth. But the real moment of truth came to him in the way he relates in chapter 19, "The Dark Night of the Suvla Landing." Standing on a height above the G. H. Q. camp, he watched a formidable convoy of destroyers, battleships, and great liners loaded with troops moving out for the surprise assault on Suvla which, it was hoped, would drive the Turks back to Constantinople. He was on duty from one to four that night to take the Intelligence telegrams, and the single important one which arrived said, "When does the next hospital ship come? This one is full." He recaptures the agony of waiting for news about the landing — and the news does not come. In the wan air of dawn, he went to bed:

It was a long time before I fell sound asleep, for I kept waking to clutch at phantoms. There was no vestige of hope left in my mind that the Suvla Landing could now succeed. I felt as if I had watched a system crash to pieces before my eyes, as if I had stood at the deathbed of an old order. The guns I could hear might have been a growling that foretold the murderous folly of the Somme. The war would last now until we had all turned ourselves into Germans to win it. An absurd phrase went singing through my head. *We have lost our amateur status to-night.* It was foolish for me who had been old enough to appreciate the muddle of the South African War to go on believing in the practical value of the public-school system. . . . Last night must somehow be separated from any other night. . . . It had been too profoundly moving an experience to melt irritably into another dusty day. It must be enshrined in sleep, and remembered all the rest of my life as a dream in which I had beheld so many other people's dreams topple over and crash. And away in London they would be getting up presently, unaware that during the night the old London had vanished.[8]

Gallipoli Memories, then, is another contribution to the epic story of the disillusionment resulting from World War I; Mackenzie tells of the end of dreams, the end of youth, the end of an age, as he experienced them.

First Athenian Memories (1931) and *Greek Memories* (1932; withdrawn and reissued in 1939) are perhaps less interesting for the general reader since Mackenzie is arguing in them for his own point of view in a very complicated political controversy. They have their exciting moments, but Mackenzie's chief desire is to set the record straight; and anyone not familiar with the history of Greece in the twentieth century may easily become lost in the story of political intrigue. King Constantine I came to the throne just before World War I; since his wife Sophie was the Kaiser's sister, and since he was convinced that Germany would win, his sympathies were clear. On the other hand, Prime Minister Venizelos was on the side of the Allies. Venizelos was forced by the King to resign in 1915; he then won an electoral victory, returned to the premiership, and negotiated an agreement for a landing at Salonica by the Allies. When he was again forced to resign in October, 1915, he then established a provisional government at Salonica and declared war against the Central Powers.

On August 14, 1915, Mackenzie, almost too sick to drag himself out of his cabin on the yacht *Imogen,* had his first sight of Greece — the marble columns of the Temple of Poseidon on Cape Sounion. In Athens, he set to work to transform a comic apology for counterespionage into an efficient operation; he established a very elaborate card-index file containing information about spies or German sympathizers, he built up an information network (the Greek porter at the German Embassy was on his payroll), and he established a system of passport control for movement to certain restricted areas. He also became a marked Venizelist supporter; he was twice shot at by Royalists while he was driving in his car; and, during the disturbance of December 1, 1916, the Greek reservists made his house look like a pepperpot and destroyed all his clothing and other belongings. In Athens, he became a semimythical figure, a bogy who appeared in his own name in a throwaway sheet called *The*

Gentleman in the Black Fez, which described a series of adventures in which he was bound and gagged and flung out of railway trains only to effect miraculous escapes.[9] And, when he left Athens, it was to invade the Cyclades and get these islands to declare themselves as on the side of the Provisional Government.

Reviewing *First Athenian Memories,* along with Sir Basil Thomson's *The Allied Secret Service in Greece* (which took the opposite side: Mackenzie said that its publication was paid for out of Royalist funds[10]), *The Times* said that the part played by the British Empire in these events was thoroughly discreditable, but that, "if one has to read about it at all, Mr. Mackenzie is at least able to make one laugh by his descriptions of the fantastic follies, absurdities, and blunders painstakingly committed by hardworking and earnest officials and diplomatists. . . ."[11] Mackenzie's basic complaint was that Britain had no policy at all; British Foreign Secretary Sir Edward Grey had in fact said that Britain had no policy in the Near East, except to use a restraining influence on the French. In Thomson's account, the Comte de Roquefeuil, the French naval attaché, is the villain with Venizelos as his puppet. Mackenzie would not dispute that the French and Italians tried to bring parts of the Eastern Mediterranean within their hegemony; but the errors, contradictions, and vacillations of his own compatriots are his main subject. He presents Venizelos as a great statesman who was hampered by the suspicion and ineptitude of those very Allied Powers whom he was trying to help.

In the Preface to *Aegean Memories* (1940) Mackenzie says that the prosecution of *Greek Memories* has given this book a somewhat different shape from its original conception; he has suppressed a certain amount of material about espionage because he cannot be bothered with more arguments about Intelligence work. Perhaps as a result, the book gives a very zestful account of the period he spent as the ruler of Syra and the other islands in the Cyclades. Though he was only a captain, he had about thirty Port Control Officers under him. Sailing about these islands in his yacht *Avlis,* he was almost a Homeric figure. The Common Council of Tenos, for example, sent him a beautifully written document expressing the island's gratitude and devotion to him and to its "great protectress England." Perhaps there is too much sense of his own importance and the correctness of his views: *"Every* suggestion I have made since I started here has been *finally* adopted and has worked well. Not a single suggestion made by anybody else but has *failed* to work well. This is simply due to the fact that I have had from the start a perfectly clear idea of what I was trying to do."[12]

When Mackenzie made a secret visit to Venizelos in Athens, and outlined the schemes he had in mind, at one point Venizelos gave him leave to continue "with the gesture of a kindly don humouring a talkative undergraduate." We hear little of Venizelos's ideas and much of Mackenzie's, which are in the vein of giving one country this and another country that. (Some of his schemes, such as one for giving Venizelos the whole coast of Asia Minor, are very flighty indeed.) Yet he is not a megalomaniac. The book is, among other things, a record of precious friendships, as with Edward Knoblock and John Hope-Johnstone, a Cambridge man who was a rival for Norman Douglas as a conversationalist. When Mackenzie was recalled from his position as director of the Aegean Intelligence Service in August, 1917, he recounts that every single officer under his command asked to be recalled with him. The work that he and his colleagues did, however, comes in almost as a footnote to the narrative of the continuous quarrels over whom he was to work with and whom he was to work under; his criticism of the base wallahs is often very well supported, even if his own views of the political developments that the United Kingdom should have supported often seem both visionary and naive.

The memorable moments in the book are associated with scenes of incomparable beauty, such as the remembrance of Rhodes: "I am standing in a sunlit gothic courtyard from which a tall palm rises to the blue sky, and I am looking at the tombstone of an English knight who died in the first years of the sixteenth century. His name has passed from my mind, but his epitaph remains. *With God, which is better.*"[13] The war brought Mackenzie many disappointments and frustrations, but for him to sail over the Aegean Sea in his own vessel and visit in reality dozens of places which had been in the forefront of his imagination ever since his Classical studies at St. Paul's was the adventure of a lifetime. Fortunately, he retained in his memory and conveys in his writing the special quality of that experience.

II   Literature in My Time

One of Mackenzie's more interesting reminiscential works was the product of a reluctant interruption to another project. His agent, Ralph Pinker, arranged for him to write a book about literature in a series that Rich and Cowan was bringing out on various subjects "in my time." "I had planned to get on with a novel to be called *The*

Darkening Green," Mackenzie writes, "and was annoyed with Pinker for landing me with a pot-boiler I was in no mood to write and in which I feared I might scald myself."[14] But Kenneth Young declares that no one interested in English writing from the 1890's to 1930 should miss *Literature in My Time.*[15] This work is of special value as a record of impressions — as of the veneration in which George Meredith was held at the turn of the century (Mackenzie, much preferring Hardy as a novelist, calls Meredith "a *faux bonhomme* of the intellect"); the emancipation which took place in the 1890's; the electric effect of Galsworthy's *Man of Property* (1906), and his success in impressing the rest of Europe, partly accounted for "by so many of Galsworthy's characters being exactly what the Continent supposes English people are"; and the resentment against romantic personalities like Robert Louis Stevenson and Rupert Brooke which obtained at the time he was writing.

Against Cyril Connolly's view that Mackenzie writes tame satire, we can set Young's that in this book he uses a deadly weapon: "Flash, flash goes Mackenzie's swordstick, and upon no writer does it light with more accuracy than upon D. H. Lawrence, whose future hope of renown would, he thought, depend on his poetry and his short stories. But for his preaching and his doctrine he has nothing but contempt."[16] Lawrence's anti-Christian obsession, Mackenzie writes, was "really based on a personal jealousy of Our Lord Jesus Christ." "His mind was as hag-ridden by sex," he continues, "as that of John Knox." By the time of *Lady Chatterley's Lover,* Lawrence's feeling of persecution had become so acute that he had lost all sense of proportion, and his "solemn printing of words which, however familiar in speech, are only written by lunatics was either comic or pathetic or both."[17]

On the other hand, Mackenzie considered James Joyce's *Ulysses* "the major piece of literature this time has witnessed." It is "the second part of *Faust* written at last, and the most convincing proof ever penned of the possibility of human damnation, the profoundest revelation of evil ever set down upon paper." And Mackenzie concludes his discussion of Joyce by a remarkable comparison of him and Lawrence: "When Lawrence sought to strip the ultimate veil from man in *Lady Chatterley's Lover* the effect was as painfully embarrassing as when an old maid suddenly goes mad and begins to shriek obscenities. That was the result of the provincial Anglo-Saxon revolting against provincial puritanism. It is the shadow of Lucifer which broods over a work like *Ulysses;* the only shadow over *Lady Chatterley's Lover* is cast by a little tin Bethel."[18]

Two things stand out in the analysis of contemporary culture which Mackenzie makes: the feeling that the classical past has been abandoned and a new barbarism has arrived, and the anticipation (in 1933) of the sexy 1960's:

Once the question of birth control becomes a topic on their belief in which candidates for Parliament can be examined by hecklers there is something a little wild in expecting that the literature of the time will not reflect such sexual preoccupation. . . . The formal abolition of any attempt at procreation can only produce an increasing moral and emotional confusion which must be reflected in literature. However, unless the novel can keep pace with the emotional processes of the mind that the present rate of material development seems likely to bring about, it will vanish, because the combination of radio and the cinema already provide for the majority all that is required in the way of mental entertainment, and with the addition of television the competition will become even more severe. The novel can only survive by its ability to offer something which nothing else can offer, and though birth-control may presently be a topic for the Children's Hour at the B. B. C., the moral and emotional confusion of a humanity which has formally rejected its own humanity will for some time yet be a prerogative of the novelist and the poet.[19]

In the dedication of *Literature in My Time* to Francis Brett Young, Mackenzie insists on the personal aspect of the book; it is not dispassionate criticism, but an intensely personal record of impressions by a writer who is concerned about literature as a reflection of the cultural and moral situation of its age.

III   My Life and Times: *Mackenzie Redivivus*

Perhaps the most striking thing about *My Life and Times* is the boldness of its plan. "It is four o'clock on the afternoon of October 16th, 1961, with the moon coming to her first quarter as I set out to write the first octave . . .," Mackenzie begins. "This octave will be published (D. V.) on my eightieth birthday in January 1963, after which I hope to write an octave a year, each one to be published on as many birthdays as I am left to keep in this world."[20] "If by God's grace I should succeed in keeping what many will think is a presumptuous timetable," he continues, "I shall be eighty-nine when the tenth octave is published in January 1972 and I shall leave the diary of an octogenarian for posthumous publication."[21] It seems quite fantastic for a man of seventy-eight to sit down to write an autobiography ten volumes long. The courage and intrepidity of the man appear even more remarkable when we realize that some years before he began this ambitious project he had had to give up writing the second part of his history of the Indian Army in World War II because he had lost the sight of one eye.

His inspiration, he admits, is self-indulgence, "or in other words to relive as much as I can of what has been a full and fortunate life."[22] John Bowen wrote concerning the third volume, " . . . Sir Compton's enjoyment in recreating it is the most powerful emotion his writing communicates."[23] And the sense of pleasure is present, Mackenzie himself shows, because he is reliving pleasant experiences. The main impression we derive from his memoirs is of his zest for life; these are the remembrances of a man for whom existence has never been dull or prosaic.

Nevertheless, Bowen, like other reviewers who referred to Mackenzie's "total recall," finds the third volume almost boring. Sir Charles Petrie writes in an otherwise laudatory review that Octave One "makes a shaky start, being a trifle overburdened with genealogical detail. . . ."[24] The first volume does, in fact, offer a good illustration of Mackenzie's refusal to reject anything which is at hand; after writing two short chapters about the first two years of his life, he inserts a thirty-six-page summary of his great-grandfather's *Thirty Years Passed among the Players in England and America.* Then follows another digression of twenty-three pages on his mother's family, the Batemans, before he comes back to himself at the age of two. As A. P. Ryan writes of a later volume, "It is packed with miscellaneous treasure trove, all jostled together anyhow as in a jackdaw's nest."[25] E. C. Beer expands on the same idea: "The reader of *My Life and Times* occasionally feels that he is about to go down in a sea of remembered particulars of food, clothes, weather, animals, houses, furniture, conversations, names and faces. . . ."[26] Conceding that Mackenzie is superb company, H. D. Ziman nevertheless protests that, by the Sixth Octave, it is the reader who is flagging: "Sir Compton seems to have kept every letter he has written or received, every press cutting and every telegram — and here they are . . . there is too much material and too little reflection. It is like the patter of a non-stop entertainer."[27]

Another possible criticism, however, is associated with what Mackenzie does *not* include: he stops short of that degree of self-revelation which has come to be expected of the contemporary autobiographer. For years his friends had been begging him to tell the story of his life; he had delayed doing so "because I did not feel I could bring myself to indulge in what amounts to undressing in public until old age had removed me far enough from the past to be able to regard that youth as somebody for whose behaviour I was no longer responsible."[28] But he does not undress in public; long and thorough as his autobiography seems, some aspects of his life do not get into it. "I know that writing as I am these Octaves in the decade of the 'sexy' sixties I am indulging in out-moded sexual reticence," he says. "However, I cannot escape from the conviction that a man does not kiss and tell. . . . I know what critics are asking for when they suggest my failure to dig down deeper into myself, but even if I wanted to make my private parts public property I should not have the nerve, even if I lived into my nineties. . . ."[29]

For the criticism he has a sufficient defense; yet, in consequence, he often gives the impression of having a prepared answer to every possible question. John Freeman came close to this objection in a television interview with Mackenzie when he said, "You are a person who has written a great deal about your reminiscences. I sometimes feel that you mostly remember what you have written, rather than having an actual vivid memory."[30] Having put Mackenzie's memory to the test, I can testify that it was amazing,[31] but he certainly has arranged his remembrances of writers like Wells and James into neatly shaped accounts which he repeats when their names come into his narrative. Regarding his controversy with Lawrence over *The Man Who Loved Islands,* for example, he mentions facetiously that Lawrence needed a lesson in botany: "He had written too beautifully about flowers to be easily forgiven for covering a granite island in the Channel with cowslips; he should know that cowslips favour lime."[32] There are considerable differences between Mackenzie's account of his experiences in *My Life and Times* and elsewhere — for example, the events in Greece during World War I are given a different emphasis from that in *First Athenian Memories* and *Greek Memories* — but still at crucial points the reader may feel that the author is not being sufficiently candid with him and is trying to fob off inquiry with a facetious remark or an amusing story.

Another possible criticism is that the autobiography may give an impression of monumental egotism. Hugo Williams refers to Mackenzie's carefully considered self-esteem and to his disingenuous nudging of every episode towards his own glory.[33] John Bowen mentions his allusions to his own good looks and his outstanding talent, his quotations from his own essays and his own poems, his dropping of names — none of which become people.[34] The criticism is partly true; Mackenzie is telling his own story, and he is presumptuous enough to think that his own life, his own impressions, and his own line of reasoning which justified his conduct to others or to himself will be of interest to his readers.

Yet it is untrue to say that he never gets outside himself and never draws a portrait of anyone else. As Young writes, "almost every well-known English writer of this century, and some of the last, step before us in their living likeness, and not writers alone but musicians, ambassadors, scientists and at least one big businessman, who is the only wholly unpleasant portrait of a real person Mackenzie paints."[35] Moreover, though he mentions the names of the eminent, Mackenzie values people for what they are in themselves. In Octave Seven, he introduces us both to Lord Lovat's family and to some of the local characters on Barra (such as the Coddie and the Crookle), and he has equal affection for both; writing of Barra he says, "Am I not to be envied for having spent so many years in close communion with such people?"[36]

Because of the decline in his reputation, Mackenzie perhaps feels a greater need to vindicate himself than most writers do; in addition, he has something of the actor's need to see himself as a public personality and to repeat the tributes which assure him that he is indeed being recognized as a member of his profession — "They loved me in Stoke-on-Trent" becomes transmuted into "They loved *The Monarch of the Glen.*" But it would take a special kind of monster to write an autobiography as long as Mackenzie's which was characterized entirely by neurotic self-absorption, and this is not the impression which *My Life and Times* gives at all.

After due attention has been paid to the various criticisms, we must observe that the reception of the autobiography has been overwhelmingly cordial. It looks "like a marathon of garrulity," writes Peter Dickinson in *Punch;* and he adds that "the pace seems a series of uncontrolled jerks, like a tumble downstairs." Nevertheless, his reaction is favorable: "And yet the effect is absorbing and very successful. This is the talk of an old man who has done things and seen people, long ago, but with an intense pleasure and interest in everything he experienced. Let him talk on."[37] And even this is a more pejorative judgment than most. Many of the reviewers chose the appearance of *My Life and Times* as an opportunity for a revaluation of Mackenzie's career; a notable example was the notice of Octave One in the *Times Literary Supplement,* headed "The Entertainer." "Let us hope that on his eightieth birthday . . . ," said the reviewer, "he, too, will at last be recognized for what he is: one of the most naturally gifted and versatile writers of the century." Such possible flaws in the first volume as the long discursions on Mackenzie's forebears and other digressions from the matter in hand are dealt with lightly, and the overall judgment is that his admirers will look forward impatiently to future octaves.[38] By Octave Seven, Walter Allen was writing in the *New York Times Book Review,* "It has been reviewed at greater length and more enthusiastically, I think, than any of the previous volumes — I suspect because we're beginning to wonder whether we've ever done justice to this remarkable man who is part of the history of our time. . . ."[39]

If Mackenzie is part of the history of our time, his autobiography is seen by many as a substantial contribution to its social history. John Raymond calls Octave One a work of superb evocation.[40] The *Times Literary Supplement* reviewer of Octave Two says that Sir Compton possesses three great virtues which make him particularly fitted to be the social historian of his period: an encyclopedic memory, an extraordinarily wide range of interests, and a deep respect for factual accuracy.[41] E. C. Beer writes of the third volume that "here . . . recaptured once and for all, is what it was like to have youth and talent and charm and hosts of friends, and to know that the world was your oyster, in good King Edward's golden days."[42] The most laudatory of these tributes is possibly that of Charles Curran, who sees Mackenzie as a Charles Greville, Thomas Creevey, Horace Walpole, and Sir Jonah Barrington rolled into one; and he asserts that " 'Octave Eight' captures to perfection the peculiar flavour — a blend of dedication and dottiness — that characterised Britain during the last war. It will last as long as anybody is interested in that period."[43]

If some of the critics, like Dickinson, make it seem that Mackenzie's narrative proceeds by jerks and jumps and if others repeat James's regretful observation that selection is not in him, a considerable number also realize that there is more art to his successful evocation of the past than many readers may suspect. Robert Speaight writes, "We are whisked hither and thither, but we always know where we are. This is part of Sir Compton's professionalism."[44] John Raymond concludes his review of Octave One by calling Mackenzie a great craftsman, and his review of Octave Four contains a similar compliment: "A Cockaigne measure, beautifully treaded."[45] Of the second volume, David Hughes comments, "No one could fault the timing and suavity of the perfor mance."[46] And the reviewer of Octave Eight in the *Times Literary Supplement* seeks for superlatives: "the author moves to the top end of his brilliant and well-tempered keyboard."[47]

None of Mackenzie's books since his early novels had received such high praise as the separate volumes of *My Life and Times*. This praise might have had a patronizing or condescending air about it, but such was not actually the case; as Auberon Waugh recognized, the books deserved something better than either attitude: "There is a terrible temptation when reviewing any book by an octogenarian to talk of dogs walking on their hinder legs. To apply this to Octave VII would not only be ill-mannered and ungrateful, but also inaccurate. Sir Compton's autobiography is absorbing. . . ."[48] *My Life and Times* both established itself as an important work and restored Mackenzie to a reputation as a serious writer. "Over thirty years ago I regretfully wrote of him as a perfectionist who had taken the wrong turning," said Raymond Mortimer in the London *Sunday Times;* and, then after a brief survey of his works, he said of his autobiography, "Indeed I have read nothing of his since 'Sinister Street' that seems so durable."[49]

CHAPTER 10

Conclusion: Unity in Diversity

I Mackenzie's Nonfictional Prose

MACKENZIE'S future reputation will depend on his novels and his memoirs, not on his essays, biographies, historical accounts, and miscellaneous other nonfictional writings. Nonetheless, these deserve some attention, if only to illustrate how his continuing preoccupations are reflected in them. Even his frankest hack work is likely to touch on one of his passionate interests and gain force and energy from doing so; he pours contempt on a cold objectivity: "What a wound contemporary historical writing has inflicted on literature. Partisanship is the breath of life for history, and the present cold circumscribed approach is one sign of the devitalisation that appears to be gradually infecting the whole of the Western world."[1] In fact, Mackenzie even describes such partisanship as psychologically healthy:

Marryat's book *[Children of the New Forest]* inspired me with a hatred for Roundheads which I retain to this day. I think it is a valuable influence on the minds of the young to hate certain historical figures because I believe it makes them less liable to hate the people with whom they come into contact through life. I can affirm that I have never hated any individuals who were still alive except Hitler and the pus of humanity he gathered. My hatred expends itself on figures of the past like Henry VII and Henry VIII, Good Queen Bess, John Knox, Oliver Cromwell, William of Orange, George I, the Butcher Cumberland, Frederick the Great and Disraeli.[2]

As we would expect, in his historical studies his judgments are biased, strong, and forthright, as this sample indicates: "It is beyond, the scope of these pages to attempt even an outline of the treacheries and bloody deeds by which a collection of the blackest villains that ever defiled the pages of history drove the Queen of Scots from her throne to find captivity and death at the hands of a queen who lacked at once the essential bodily and mental characteristics of woman-hood."[3]

Yet the book from which this is taken, *Catholicism and Scotland* (1936), is much better than two other Scottish studies, *Prince Charlie* (1932) and *Prince Charlie and his Ladies* (1934); and it is of considerable intrinsic importance. Mackenzie is rebutting such views as that of Dr. A. J. Campbell: "When the Scottish Reformers carried through the Scottish Reformation they did not regard themselves as pulling down an old Church and setting up a new Church in its place."[4] Campbell is trying to make good Covenanters of the Cistercians, says Mackenzie wrily; against this view of the special character of Scottish Christianity, he argues for its affinities with the rest of Latin Christendom. An implication of his book is stressed in a review of it in *Blackfriars:* "As an essay it possesses a considerable and perhaps a permanent value, for it helps to emphasize that there can be no necessary conflict between Catholicism and Scottish nationalism. In Scotland, as in France and Ireland, Catholicism may stress rather than erase the traits of a purely national culture."[5] So the book underlines, as for example, does *The Four Winds,* Mackenzie's persistent concern for the preservation of national identities together with his belief that, if there is a place for internationalism, it is in the domain of religion.

Similar emphases are found in his books on another of his passionate enthusiasms, Greece. For a series on "Great Occasions," he wrote in 1934 an account of Marathon and Salamis in which he pointed out that an internationalist like H. G. Wells could contend that the defeat of the Persians was a disaster for the human race since it meant "balkanization," a victory for the noxious theory of nationalism. With some irony, Mackenzie agrees that the Greek victory did postpone internationalism: "Centralization and bureaucracy would have afflicted or benefitted western humanity over so long a period that the machine age might have arrived centuries before it did."[6] Similarly, in a study of Pericles (1937), he detects some quality in the bright Hellenic air which kindles in men's minds the suspicion of tyranny, the fear of a single man's domination. He also points to a historical parallel: as Athens was ruined by her failure to follow the strategy of Pericles, so modern Greece was brought close to ruin by her failure to follow the strategy of Venizelos. Having only scanty material on Pericles' life to work with, Mackenzie eked out his material with a good deal of background information, a digression on the Elgin Marbles and the morality of keeping them in the British Museum, and the story of Socrates' military campaign.

Wind of Freedom (1943) dealt with the Greek resistance to Hitler, so that he had a heroic tale to tell; and Laurence Durrell wrote to compliment him on giving "the one really properly documented account of this confused, marvellous and miraculous business."[7] On the other hand, *Greece in My Life* (1960), written after he spent seven weeks in Greece in the autumn of 1958 working on three television films for the B. B. C., is patchy and disappointing, though once more the special character of the Hellenes and the value of the Balkans as an escape from the shoal in which the foreigner swims are given particular emphasis.

In two biographies — *Mr. Roosevelt* (1943) and *Dr. Benes* (1946) — which derived their inspiration from wartime conditions, we again see the merging of Mackenzie's political and religious views. He wrote a hero-worshipping life of Franklin D. Roosevelt in 1943, showing him as a man of destiny: "Roosevelt and Hitler are engaged upon an evolutionary struggle: they are fighting for the spirit of man." The book is hastily written and has obvious faults, but it establishes a contrast between American and British government which is of considerable interest: Mackenzie traces the special character of the American system to a theory of social contract which Jefferson incorporated in the Declaration of Independence, but he sees Britain as governed by an oligarchy which has usually known when to surrender to the demands of liberalism. Against Hitler's claim for the historical role of the German people, he sees purpose in history in the following terms: "Democracy puts a strain upon the faith of humanity which can become unendurable in hours of disillusionment. Yet democracy, which provides the only rational view of a Divine political purpose, has survived so many assaults from without, so much undermining from within, that to deny the possibility of ever attaining the goal towards which it moves so slowly, so painfully, and sometimes so disgracefully, is to declare all the years of recorded history more useless than a heap of dead leaves and to offer them as a bonfire to the destructive and evil spirit of misdirected evolution."[8]

In *Mr. Roosevelt,* Mackenzie criticizes a pro-Soviet article in the *New Statesman;* and he refers satirically to the agile feat of mental acrobatics which Communists had to perform when Hitler's attack on the Union of Soviet Socialist Republics transformed what they had been sabotaging as an Imperialism war into a crusade. Yet in

Dr. Benes he associates himself with Benes in rejoicing that all the difficulties between Russia and Poland have been removed; and he composes a very sentimental picture of a fireside chat between Stalin and Benes: "On one occasion we were talking about Stalin, for whom Dr. Benes has a shrewd admiration and, as I surmise, a warm affection, and I had a momentary vision of these men as two countrymen on either side of a fire discussing a deal in corn or cattle and chaffing one another as camouflage for the mutual respect they felt for one another as sharp men of business."[9] A special irony attaches to this smiling picture of the gruff but kindly dictator, and to the role of mediator between East and West for which Benes casts Czechoslovakia in the book, when one remembers that the Communist coup and the defeat and death of Benes took place within two years of the book's publication.

Nevertheless, some of Mackenzie's principal ideas find expression here, in particular the value of small states and the necessity of preserving their political and cultural integrity, and the association between religion and political liberty. This connection is emphasized by Benes in a long explanation of how he returned to religious belief after abandoning it; he thought that the respect of one human being for another had to depend upon an absolute standard of behavior and therefore to have a religious sanction:

... I came to the conclusion ... that Fascism in Italy and Nazism in Germany, the terrible European depression, the fight for Communism, and all the manifold strife and struggle of the post-war years resulted from the people of the twentieth century being in disharmony with themselves. They were mentally sick; they had lost not only their faith but their ideals. Such happiness as they enjoyed was the gratification of their material desires in a world without moral standards. Such a conception of life was an example of the decline of true democracy, which, dependent as it is upon man's continuous moral development, requires absolute standards of religion.[10]

Most men are convinced of their own political wisdom, and perhaps Mackenzie is erroneously convinced that in the major issues of the century he has usually had reason on his side. He has either flirted with or passionately espoused some very odd causes. Yet, from a wide variety of experiences — his classical studies, his conversion, his adventures in war, his conflicts with bureaucrats, his association with Scottish Nationalists, his experience of living among the people of Capri and the people of Barra — he has fashioned a coherent and harmonious set of opinions concerning the minimum requirements for the good life. Has he preached his views *ad nauseam?* In our times, they could bear repeating. But he has undoubtedly conveyed them most successfully, not through the direct statement of his nonfiction but through the indirection of his comic novels.

II *Mackenzie's Stature as a Novelist*

In a radio broadcast entitled "Broken Promise" (which he delivered in 1959) Angus Wilson discussed the English novel between 1912 and 1922; and he gave special attention to three of the novelists selected by Henry James as promising — Mackenzie, Gilbert Cannan, and Hugh Walpole — and to a fourth whom he added himself, J. D. Beresford. It is perhaps difficult to read these novelists now, Wilson said, if we think of the flood of circulating-library fiction which has come after them; but he conceded to them freshness, conviction, and above all a serious attempt to present the reality of experience. Nevertheless, the experience of going through their works was like going down a great middle road which so broadened and sprawled as it tried to take in the whole of life by a painless process that it might have gone outside the realm of art entirely.

Romantic or Realistic (and on the whole they thought that a judicious mixture best represented life), these novelists thought of their task as ever-expandable. One result was a lack of form; life just flowed on, and so did their novels with the element of selection becoming smaller and smaller: "There is so very much to say and so little time to say it, that inevitably the writing must be left to take care of itself. After all, the divine spark worked overtime with the great novelists of the past, and the less it is interfered with by conscious processes, the more likely it is to make sudden, wonderful flashes again." Abandoning irony for the moment, Wilson indicated the dangers involved in the sequence novels which they all wrote: "The conscious attempt to capture life whole and vibrant is a will-o'-the-wisp, an evasive vision that naturally lures onwards the young writer with a seemingly bottomless store of energy to draw on." Characters appeared again and again, "until the whole edifice of the contemporary novel is burrowed through and through like a vast rabbit warren. And the more the characters overflowed and multiplied, the less substantial and lifelike they became."

The desire to include the whole of life meant that these writers had to be absolutely up to date; all the new influences — flapper daughters and Bolshie sons, Oedipus complexes, the new morality, strikes and wartime bloodshed — had to come into their novels. Nevertheless, the note they sounded was one of reassurance; after all, they were dealing with the same plucky old world which novelists had been portraying for the last hundred years, and they presented a picture of life which was eminently acceptable to the great middle-class reading public. "No group of writers, perhaps, were so electic in their choice of ideas, so receptive of fresh fruits; yet few serious writers so ceaselessly boiled and pulped them down into the same tasteless dish."[11]

As regards Mackenzie, the indictment is in many ways just; although many of the criticisms are familiar, many of them are also deserved. The great nineteenth-century French writer who tried to bring the whole life of his country within the scope of his fiction, Balzac won admiration for the boldness of his conception and for the courage with which he faced its incredible complexity. His fiftieth or hundredth imitator, however, is not likely to inspire the same awe. Wilson's worry about the sequence novels as a will-o'-the wisp which the writer will never have enough energy to catch hardly applies to Mackenzie; he had enough energy to plan and execute not one but several sagas. The very notion of a sequence or saga is perhaps inartistic, however, since it means that the writer conceives of his work as the somewhat mechanical completion of a task planned years in advance: he is willing to sacrifice the imaginative vision which might lure him to treat of other subjects during that period of time. It is one thing to be professional, but it is another to put the creative imagination in chains.

As we go down the sprawling middle road constructed by these novelists, Wilson says, it may be difficult for us to remember that we are in the realm of art at all. The novel, to change the metaphor, seems to be a comfortable sloppy vessel which can hold anything which comes along and which mocks the disciplined selectivity which must be used for other genres. Mackenzie wrote so much, and left out so little, that he seems particularly vulnerable to Wilson's ironic references about letting the writing take care of itself and relying on the divine spark which has helped so many writers in the past to visit him if the conscious mind did not get in its way. Wilson's criticism of the sameness of his four novelists, their boiling everything down into the same tasteless dish, was amusingly anticipated by Katherine Fullerton Gerould in her "British Novelists, Ltd." (1918). She treated Mackenzie, Walpole, Beresford, Oliver Onions, and W. L. George as members of a syndicate and made conjectures about their assignments — which one was supposed to cover murder, which one the Empire, which one female psychology?

"For the outstanding fact," she declared, "is that they all write alike; that they deal in the same characters, the same backgrounds, and the same situations, and that they have the same point of view." "Mr. Mackenzie," she went on, "forces his vocabulary as the others do not (he prides himself, I fancy, particularly on the number of his metaphors for the moon); but apart from Mr. Mackenzie's occasional exoticism, they write alike."[12] Wilson's complaint about rabbit-warrening had also been anticipated by P. P. Howe in an article on "Fiction and Perpetual Life" in 1919: "The total effect of Mr. Mackenzie's fiction is not to lead us to believe that there have been about five people in the world and that they are dead — as a caustic writer once said was the effect of Classical Education — but rather to lead us to believe that there are about five people in the world at present and that nothing in the world can kill them."[13]

When we see that Wilson's strictures on Mackenzie virtually repeat criticisms made three decades earlier, his description of Mackenzie's broken promise seems to take on a special authenticity and definitiveness: Mackenzie seems accurately "placed." But the more we examine Wilson's discussion, the more we realize that it is a bright, breezy, but not entirely reliable survey of the broad middle road with which it purports to deal. Even in the period between 1912 and 1922, is Mackenzie always so reassuring as Wilson wants us to believe? That public-school life is a depressing straightjacket, that the Empire is a fraud, that a theatrical career means a monotonous round of boring and meaningless activity, that young love is deceptive and heartbreaking, that the war to end wars was a horrible fiasco — these are some of the supposedly reassuring themes with which Mackenzie dealt in his early novels. Was it the same plucky old, amusing old world with which novelists had been dealing since Dickens's time? Mackenzie's Michael Fane was obsessed with the necessity for turning it upside down; his story culminated in his violent rejection of the status quo. Was Wilson right when he said that his group of writers always wrote the same novel or the same kind of novel — a sloppy, undisciplined kind? As we have seen, Mackenzie tried a number of very interesting technical experiments, such as the device of never letting the central character off the page in *Carnival* and that of keeping the point of view as close as possible to that of the hero in *Sinister Street*. Undoubtedly, *Sylvia and Michael* provided the critics with a horrible example of a sprawling plot, but they should have remembered that Mackenzie rarely let himself go as he did in this novel.

In his book on *The Fictional Technique of Scott Fitzgerald,* James E. Miller, Jr., recalls the distinction Henry James made in his article discussing Mackenzie between saturation and selection, the slice of life and the extract from life — "the extract flasked and fine." Miller sees the distinction as important in connection with his subject: *This Side of Paradise* is in the tradition of saturation and is modeled on Mackenzie; but *The Great Gatsby,* though written.only five years later, is vastly superior because it is in the tradition of selection and modeled on Joseph Conrad. Miller, who considers *Sinister Street* the most saturated of all saturation novels, discusses it in terms of James's reference to the lively talent of the memorizer and of Mackenzie's reply in his "Epilogical Letter to Mavro-gordato": "If I were to set down all I could remember of my child-hood, the book would not by this time have reached much beyond my fifth year." Mackenzie seems to be arguing, Miller observes, that because he could have put more in and did not, he must have used selection; but this suggests the use of omission or addition rather than of a fictional method. Following James, Miller looks for the theme of *Sinister Street,* and he is dissatisfied with Mackenzie's statement that it deals with the youth of a man who will presumably be a priest: "But how, one might well ask, is the theme differentiated from the story; what is the basis of relevance established by this broad statement of the theme?"[14]

Before we reply, it is worth noting that, if Miller takes Mackenzie as the supreme example of saturation, James does not.[15] James begins his discussion of "The Younger Generation" by conceding that saturation has certain merits: it involves a sharp specification of the human scene, an immersion in it, a temporary mastering of our sensibility. Nevertheless, we are bound to question what it ac-complishes: "Yes, but is this *all*? Where is the interest?" These writers "squeeze out to the utmost the plump and more or less juicy orange of a particular acquainted state and let this affirmation of energy, however directed or undirected, constitute for them the 'treatment' of the theme." In Bennett (James is not quite fair to *The Old Wives' Tale),* the sole inference we can make is that things go on and on; Gilbert Cannan gives us constatations pure and simple; Wells gives us the experience of his own mind — the composition is "about" his own adventure; Walpole is entirely happy with satura-tion and looks for nothing else. So we search for the supreme reference that will avert the bankruptcy of the senses, and all we find is the attempt of the slice of life to butter itself thick!

But when James turns to Mackenzie, he regards him as a rather perplexing addition to his list of saturationists. He is not a simple case, but a mystifying one; in fact, he possesses the attraction of complexity. It is not easy to say if the selective sense is not operating in *Carnival,* even if the overflooded surface would at first lead us to suspect otherwise. The novel seems a slice of life, yet it is an "extract" in the sense of not losing its center, which is its fidelity to the one question of Jenny's dolefully embarrassing little measure of life. As to *Sinister Street,* youth is clearly Mackenzie's saturation, yet the novel breathes the air of the extract in certain rounded episodes. James waits for the second part of *Sinister Street* before deciding what the novel is "about," but in the meantime he observes of it and *Carnival* that "certain betrayals of a controlling idea and a pointed intention do comparatively gleam out of the two fictions last named."[16]

Miller does not find the pointed intention present; he is right in saying that Mackenzie's explanation does not give a sufficiently precise indication of the theme of *Sinister Street,* but he is unwilling to look beyond Mackenzie's statement to see what the novel actually does. And it *does* have a theme. Analyzing the story, we saw that the experiences recounted in it work indirectly on the hero to make him redefine the concept of the gentleman and to adopt a radical stance towards his society. In the Oxford section particularly, the novel seems to "squeeze out to the utmost the plump and more or less juicy orange of a particular acquainted state," but our inference is not, or should not be, that things merely go on and on; instead, we should see such experiences as formative and predictive. Apparently random happenings act subtly to turn a boy into a man with a mature point of view.

Although Mackenzie is undeniably a saturationist, there is more to be said for this tradition than James and Miller indicate. Dealing with *The Old Wives' Tale,* James discusses the separation of the two sisters early in life and their reunion late in life: "The divided current flows together again, and the chronicle closes with the simple drying up determined by the death of the sisters. That is all; the canvas is covered, ever so closely and vividly covered, by the exhibition of innumerable small facts and aspects, at which we assist with the most comfortable sense of their substantial truth."[17] But that is not by any means all, for James neglects to note that in the last part, significantly entitled "What Life Is," Sophia and Constance come to diametrically opposed conclusions: Sophia decides that not for anything on earth would she live her life over again; and Constance accepts her fate with the invincible common sense of a sound nature. When we think we have Constance fully accounted for, in terms of heredity and environment and of following the common pattern of disillusionment and death, something eludes, some nobility of character rises above circumstance — to impress not only us but the author, who does not give the sense (as James says) of firm manipulation of his material but of standing back in awe, of wondering and questioning.

But possibly a more eminent practitioner of saturationism will serve to elucidate the uses of the technique; G. S. Fraser writes of Proust:

Proust's great theme is what the French call *recueillement,* which means more than the English 'recollection'; rather, the replucking in memory of the flowers that time has plucked already; the re-gathering, re-patterning, re-embroidering, of all the loose and ravelled threads of one's life. Life is never still, yet it is easy enough, at any calm time, for a man to number over in his mind some of the main incidents of his life; it is much more difficult to relive them contemplatively, to recapture the sense of what past time was, what in essence it still *is*. It is more difficult still to get that recaptured and revived awareness of the past into perspective with the present. . . . We are not so sure that we want to be so completely submerged into the warm and viscous depths of somebody else's life; we become oppressed at having to surrender, again and again, to all the temptations and vices that beset a young man of weak and yielding sensibility, but then we find the sensibility controlled, at least at the level of art and recollection, by a persistent organizing will and a powerful analysing intellect. The material, however, questionable in itself, is being shaped towards some generalization about love, about selfishness and insincerity, about man's experience of time, which will at least seem to have the validity of mathematics.[18]

It is a common impression that Mackenzie's love of detail gets out of control in his novels — the talent of the memorizer is too much in evidence. Yet it is clear in *Sinister Street* and *The Four Winds* that the details are intended to make the reader feel the mood of 1900 or 1910, to make him relive the experiences which a person of lively sensibility underwent, and to cause him to understand how that person's responses contributed to the shaping of his outlook on the present. We miss in Mackenzie the persistent organizing will and the powerful analyzing intellect; yet we understand that, as in Bennett and

Proust, something is being said about man's experience of time (and especially of the disappointing experience of living in the twentieth century), something which is the expression of a highly individual outlook upon the modern world.

We cannot disagree with such opinions as that of Gordon Hall Gerould, expressed in 1942, in *The Patterns of English and American Fiction,* that Mackenzie has been the victim of his ambition and of his almost unparalleled fluency.[19] But the partially related inference that he surrendered all attempts at serious and disciplined writing in the 1920's is entirely wrong. To the other examples of firm and taut fiction which we have seen, we might add a novel dealing with a homosexual politician, *Thin Ice,* (1956) which he wrote when he was in his seventies. The story is filtered through the consciousness of George Gaymer, a dilettante with an assured income who describes himself as only a feeble candle to illuminate his friend Henry Fortescue. George is, however, almost as much a center of interest as Henry; for we observe his admiration for a potential Empire builder, his bewilderment at someone whose propensities are so different from his own, his confidence that Henry will concentrate on a political future and use discretion, and his dismay when Henry finds himself passed over for political office, throws away caution, and leaves himself open to blackmail and violence. The device of the narrator enables Mackenzie to distance himself from the story — there are none of his opinions about homosexuality, there is no crude sensationalism, there is only a story of waste leading to a death in the blitz which can be considered as merciful. Some of the implications of Henry's pattern of life are made clear, as when the death of his brother and his nephew imply the end of an ancient and honorable family; but Mackenzie gives us only enough detail to establish his setting and situation firmly: the principle of selection is clearly apparent here. We must have a great deal of admiration for an elderly author who shows such self-restraint.

As we saw at the beginning of this survey, Edmund Wilson has said that "nobody is able to bring himself to give Mackenzie credit for being the fine artist that at his best he is." If we now ask what Mackenzie has done to be remembered in literary history, we can answer that, besides writing a notable autobiography, he has written successful novels in a variety of types. He has been a kind of English Proust, evoking the moods of past time. He has written some of the funniest novels in the language. And he has also managed to rein in his exuberance and his delight in invention to write novels which are admirably taut, controlled, and disciplined. Wilson complains, "But now people — not I, however — laugh their heads off over P. G. Wodehouse and pretend to take him seriously as a writer and speak with respect of Somerset Maugham, a bad writer with none of Mackenzie's distinction, when they have often never heard of Mackenzie."[20] Wilson has reason for complaint; Mackenzie should be better known.

Most of his writing, in whatever form, reflects his own unusual outlook on the world. An excellent statement of his principles can be found in his rectorial address at Glasgow University in 1932.[21] It was the centenary of Goethe, "the last human being great enough to live with the world for his background, yet one who was never under the necessity of moving farther away than Italy from the small German principality where he spent most of his life." When Mackenzie rhetorically asked whether a genius like Goethe could exist today, he answered his own question negatively: "Why, a genius of ten times the demonic force of Goethe would evaporate in the conditions of modern life." Yet the potential life of man, he thought, was richer than it had ever been: "Rapidity of transport, the prospect of longer life, a higher standard of comfort, a decrease in contagious diseases, extended opportunity for education and entertainment, these . . . are the lavish gifts of progress. . . ."

But Mackenzie thought that progress had taken a wrong turn; it was destroying the individual's sense of his own identity and importance: "nobody in posterity will be able to call his soul his own; but that will not greatly matter, because then it will have definitely [been] established that nobody possesses such an exclusively personal piece of property." To some, the standardization of national and individual characteristics was a small price to pay for the march of civilization, but to Mackenzie that standardization would render any advancement illusory: "The present threat to ultimate perfection is the too ready sacrifice of backward or imperfect parts to achieve a premature centralization which when achieved will diffuse not life but death. Nationalism is a demand by the soul of man to afford him leisure for the contemplation of his own destiny, to restore to him a richer personal life, and by narrowing his background to enable him to recover a measure of trust in his own significance in time and space." From *The Passionate Elopement* in 1911 to the last volumes of *My Life and Times* in the 1970's, Mackenzie's writing eloquently defended the soul of man against the various threats against it brought by successive decades of the twentieth century.

Notes and References

Preface

1. Henry James's articles on "The Younger Generation" appeared in the *Times Literary Supplement* on March 19 and April 2, 1914. They were extended and revised for book publication. See Leon Edel and Gordon N. Ray, eds., *Henry James and H. G. Wells: A Record of their Friendship, their Debate on the Art of Fiction, and their Quarrel* (London, 1958). I vary James's metaphor.

2. Ernest A. Baker, *A History of the English Novel* (London, 1938), X, p. 327; William York Tindall, *Forces in Modern British Literature, 1884-1946* (New York, 1949), pp. 179 and 328; G. S. Fraser, *The Modern Writer and his World* (Harmondsworth, Middlesex; 1964), p. 111.

3. Lionel Stevenson, *The English Novel: A Panorama* (Cambridge, Mass.; 1960), p. 454.

4. Edmund Wilson, London *Sunday Times,* September 2, 1962, p. 21; *New Yorker,* June 2, 1962, 121-22; also in *The Bit Between My Teeth* (London: W. H. Allan, 1965).

5. *Ibid.*

6. Walter Allen, "London Letter," *New York Times Book Review,* March 3, 1968, p. 20.

7. Compton Mackenzie, *My Life and Times* (London, 1963-), III, 40. In subsequent references, this work is identified by the word "Octave" and the relevant volume number.

8. Octave I, p. 16.

9. Octave I, p. 13.

10. Octave IV, pp. 111-12.

11. Charles Curran, "Barrage from Barra's Laird," London *Sunday Telegraph,* February 2, 1969, p. 10.

12. Sheila Kaye-Smith, "Compton Mackenzie and his Work," *The Bookman* (New York), LXII (December, 1925), 391.

Chapter One

1. *My Life and Times,* Octave 1 (London, 1963), p. 34.

2. Norman Bentwich, "A Public School's Boys-of-Letters," *Contemporary Review,* CXCVIII (1960), 435.

3. Octave II, p. 248.

4. *Ibid.,* p. 242

5. Mortimer R. Proctor, *The English University Novel* (Berkeley, 1957), p. 154.

6. Octave VII, p. 34.

7. Octave III, pp. 277-78.

8. *Ibid.,* p. 294.

9. *Ibid.,* p. 239.

10. Octave IV, pp. III-12.

11. *Gallipoli Memories* (London, 1929), pp. 15-16; Octave IV, p. 247.

12. *The Letters of F. Scott Fitzgerald,* ed. Andrew Turnbull (London, 1963), p. 356.

13. Octave V, p. 247.

14. Theodore Roy Erlandson, "A Critical Study of Some Early Novels (1911-1920) of Sir Compton Mackenzie," unpublished Ph. D. dissertation, University of Southern California, 1965, p. 370.

15. Douglas Goldring, *Reputations: Essays in Criticism* (New York, 1920), p. 51.

16. Octave V, p. 146.

17. This is a satirical story. Norman Douglas writes of Lawrence,

He was one of those mortals to whom one must never show kindness unless one wants to be stabbed in the back afterwards. I have given an example of this in *Looking Back,* and here is one of several more. The Compton Mackenzies had imprudently gone out of their way to make Lawrence happy and comfortable on Capri. They were rewarded in due course by the publication of two short stories about themselves and their household, both scurrilous and one of them libellous into the bargain.

(Experiments [London, 1946], p. 53).

The other story was "Two Blue Birds"; in her reminiscences, Faith Compton Mackenzie tells of dining alone with Lawrence on Capri and, responding to the wine and his sensitive understanding, telling him some of the secrets of her heart: "Unfortunately some months later a short story appeared in one of the popular magazines which he could not have written if I had not dined with him that night in Capri. A malicious caricature of Monty [Mackenzie], and a monstrous perversion of facts, yet the source of it clearly recognisable." (*More Than I Should* [London, 1940], p. 34.) Both stories first appeared in *The Dial* in 1927: "Two Blue Birds" in April, and "The Man Who Loved Islands" in July. The latter was announced as a separate publication by Heinemann in 1929, but Mackenzie forced its withdrawal by threatening an action for libel. It is among the more widely discussed of Lawrence's short stories; see especially Anthony West, *D. H. Lawrence* (London, 1950); F. R. Leavis, *D. H. Lawrence: Novelist* (London, 1955); Kingsley Widmer, *The Art of Perversity: D. H. Lawrence's Shorter Fiction,* (Seattle, 1962); Frederick R. Karl, "Lawrence's The Man Who Loved

Islands: The Crusoe Who Failed," in Harry T. Moore, *A D. H. Lawrence Miscellany* (Carbondale, Illinois, 1959), pp. 265-79; Julian Moynahan, *The Deed of Life* (Princeton, 1963); and George Ford, *Double Measure: A Study of the Novels and Stories of D. H. Lawrence* (New York, 1965). Ford's analysis is especially intriguing because, after calling it one of the most puzzling stories Lawrence ever wrote (the difficulty residing in identifying the tone and observing how the tone functions), he suggests that it is really a portrait of Lawrence himself.

18. Octave V, p. 257.

19. Octave VII, p. 197.

20. Val Gielgud in a program note on a radio play by Mackenzie, "Lucy Arnold," in the *Radio Times,* November 17, 1966, p. 45.

Chapter Two

1. Kenneth Young, *Compton Mackenzie,* Writers and their Work Series, No. 202 (London, 1968), p. 6.

2. Interview of the present writer with Mackenzie, January 24, 1967.

3. Reginald Auberon, *The Nineteen Hundreds* (London, 1922), quoted in Erlandson, p. 64.

4. Leo Robertson, *Compton Mackenzie: An Appraisal* (London, 1954), p. 59.

5. The long first chapter (67 pages) of Erlandson's thesis analyzes this novel in great detail.

6. *Echoes* (London, 1954), p. 94.

7. *The Passionate Elopement* (London, 1911), p. 293.

8. *Ibid.,* p. 301.

9. Douglas Goldring, *Reputations* (New York, 1920), p. 42.

10. See Erlandson, pp. 15-61.

11. *Ibid.,* pp. 18-21.

12. *Ibid.,* 34-35.

13. Anonymous review in the London *Daily News,* Feb. 8, 1911, quoted in Erlandson, p. 40.

14. *The Passionate Elopement,* p. 293.

15. Stendhal, *The Red and the Black,* trans. by Lloyd C. Parks (New York, 1970), p. 507.

16. *The Passionate Elopement,* p. 293.

17. Erlandson, p. 16.

18. *The Passionate Elopement,* p. 297.

19. Faith Compton Mackenzie, *More Than I Should* (London, 1940), p. 227.

20. Erlandson, p. 44.

21. Octave III, p. 155.

22. Cyril Connolly, *Enemies of Promise,* Penguin Modern Classics (Harmondsworth, 1961 [1938]), p. 18.

23. *Ibid.,* pp. 24-25.

24. *Ibid.,* p. 26.
25. *Ibid.,* pp. 41-42.
26. *Literature in My Time* (London, 1933), p. 129.
27. *Ibid.,* p. 95.
28. Octave III, pp. 235-36.
29. Octave IV, pp. 107-08.
30. Octave IV, p. 123.
31. *Carnival* (London, 1912), p. 34.
32. *Ibid.,* p. 90.
33. *Ibid.,* pp. 106-07.
34. *Ibid.,* p. 204.
35. Octave III, pp. 265 and 269.
36. *Literature in My Time,* p. 170.
37. Kenneth Young, *Compton Mackenzie,* p. 13.

Chapter Three

1. Octave IV, p. 153.
2. Epilogical Letter to John Mavrogordato, *Sinister Street,* Volume Two London, 1914), p. iii.
3. Mortimer R. Proctor, *The English University Novel* (Berkeley, 1957), p. 154.
4. Octave IV, p. 154.
5. *Sinister Street* (London, 1949), p. xi.
6. *Sinister Street,* (London, 1913), pp. 1-2. Mackenzie was not able to complete the novel in time for its publication as a whole in the autumn of 1913, so that it appeared in two volumes. The first was published on Sept. 1, 1913, and the second not until November 11, 1914, with the pagination carrying on from the first to the second. Appleton's, the American publishers, complicated matters still farther by changing the title of the first volume to *Youth's Encounter* and bringing out the second under the title *Sinister Street* — without explaining that the two books constituted one novel.
7. *Ibid.,* p. 159.
8. *Ibid.,* pp. 660-61.
9. Marvin Magalaner and Richard M. Kain, *Joyce: The Man, the Work, the Reputation* (New York, 1962 [1956]), p. 135.
10. *Letters of Arnold Bennett,* ed. James Hepburn. Vol. I: Letters to J. B. Pinker. (London, 1966), p. 218.
11. Evelyn Waugh, *Ronald Knox* (London, 1959), p. 126.
12. S. N. Behrman, *Portrait of Max* (New York, 1960), pp. 287-88.
13. Foreword to the 1949 edition of *Sinister Street,* p. x.
14. Erlandson, *Critical Study,* p. 171 and pp. 189-194.
15. Edmund Wilson, *The Shores of Light: A Literary Chronicle of the Twenties and Thirties* (New York, 1952), p. 28. In *The Fictional Technique of Scott Fitzgerald,* James E. Miller, Jr., discusses the influence of Macken-

zie on Fitzgerald in terms of James's distinction between the novel of saturation and the novel of selection, so that, if *This Side of Paradise* exhibits Fitzgerald drunk with Compton Mackenzie, *The Great Gatsby* shows him sobered up by Henry James.

16. Erlandson, pp. 194-5.

17. *Sinister Street,* p. 208.

18. Erlandson, p. 208.

19. See Erlandson, p. 220. The review appeared on the day of publication, Sept. 1, 1913.

20. *Sinister Street,* p. 70.

21. *Ibid.*p. 385.

22. *Ibid.,* p. 415.

23. *Ibid.,* p. 673.

24. *Ibid.,* p. 320.

25. *Ibid.,* p. 739.

26. Octave I, p. 194.

27. Both are quoted in Erlandson, pp. 160 and 202. Ford's review of the novel appeared in *The Outlook;* Shorter's comments appeared in "A Literary Letter" in *The Sphere,* LX (January 23, 1915), 110.

28. Erlandson, p. 232.

Chapter Four

1. *Literature in My Time,* p. 186. The "Theatre of Youth," the *roman fleuve,* and the sequence novel are discussed in Erlandson, pp. 132-46.

2. *Literature in My Time,* pp. 187-88.

3. Michael Sadleir, "Long Novels," *London Mercury,* XX (September, 1929), 507; quoted and discussed in Erlandson, pp. 133-34.

4. J. W. Beach, *The Twentieth Century Novel* (New York, 1932), p. 246.

5. *Literature in My Time,* p. 119; see also Octave III, pp. 26-27.

6. Octave V, p. 134.

7. Foreword to new edition of *Sinister Street* (London, 1949), p. xi.

8. *Ibid.*

9. Michael Arlen, *The Green Hat* (London, 1924), p. 24.

10. Quoted in Erlandson, p. 284.

11. Anonymous Review in the *Evening Standard* (London), Sept. 27, 1915, quoted in Erlandson, p. 256.

12. Erlandson, p. 253.

13. *Guy and Pauline* (London, 1915), p. 324.

14. *Ibid.,* p. 327.

15. Erlandson, p. 269.

16. Octave IV, p. 234.

17. Frank Swinnerton, *The Georgian Literary Scene* (London, 1938 [1935]), p. 313.

18. Octave V, p. 125; Kenneth Young, *Compton Mackenzie,* pp. 15-16.

19. Letter of Frieda Lawrence to Mackenzie, April, 1920, quoted in Octave V, pp. 176-77.

20. *Ibid.*, p. 178. The letter is dated "May 10 or 11," 1920.

21. *The Early Life and Adventures of Sylvia Scarlett* (London, 1918), p. 125

22. Octave V, p. 121.

23. In the anthology edited by Louis Kronenberger, *Novelists on Novelists* (Garden City, N. Y., 1962).

24. Leo Robertson, *Compton Mackenzie,* p. 96.

25. Alexander A. Parker, *Literature and the Delinquent: The Picaresque Novel in Spain and Europe 1599-1753* (Edinburgh, 1967), pp. 3-4.

26. R. W. B. Lewis, *The Picaresque Saint* (Philadelphia, 1961), pp. 31-33.

27. Parker, *Literature and the Delinquent,* p. 6.

28. See Miriam Allott, *Novelists on the Novel* (London, 1959), pp. 128 and 115.

29. Douglas Goldring, *Reputations* (London, 1920), pp. 50-51, discussed in Erlandson, *Critical Study,* p. 328.

30. Miriam Allott, *Novelists on the Novel,* pp. 312 and 322.

31. Octave V, p. 121. He made the reference to 10,000 telegrams in a television interview. See "Sir Compton Mackenzie 'Face to Face,' " *Listener,* LXVII (January 25, 1962), 166.

32. Octave V, p. 126.

33. Erlandson, pp. 356 ff.

34. Octave V, pp. 125-6.

35. Erlandson, p. 359.

36. The reviews in *The Nation* and *The New Statesman* both appeared on September 7, 1918; they are quoted in Erlandson, p. 360.

37. "Our Booking Office," *Punch,* CLVIII (1920), p. 399.

38. *The Early Adventures of Sylvia Scarlett,* p. 246.

39. *The Vanity Girl* (London, 1920), pp. 203-04.

40. Katherine Mansfield, "Mr. Mackenzie's Treat," *Novels and Novelists,* ed., J. Middleton Murray (London, 1930), p. 187. This review first appeared in *The Athenaeum* on May 14, 1920.

41. Erlandson notes (p. 389) that Wodehouse's *Psmith* was published in 1910, but Jeeves and Bertie Wooster did not make their appearance until 1924. He cites W. Macqueen-Pope's reference in *Carriages at Eleven* (London, 1949), p. 105, to George Grossmith's clever stage portrayals of "The rather inane, stupid young man about town of the period . . . " Erlandson's discussion of the "Bright Young Things" is on pages 395-96.

42. *The Early Adventures of Sylvia Scarlett,* p. 273.

43. *The Vanity Girl,* p. 256.

44. Katherine Mansfield, "Mr. Mackenzie's Treat," p. 187.

45. The *Observer* review appeared on May 16, 1920, and that in the *Westminster Gazette* on May 12. Both are quoted in Erlandson, p. 398.

Chapter Five

1. Compton Mackenzie, "Francis Brett Young," *The Bookman* (London), LI (August, 1920), 638.

2. Octave V, p. 147.

3. Octave V, p. 150.

4. Douglas Goldring, *Reputations: Essays in Criticism* (London, 1920), p. 51. Erlandson discusses the effect of *Poor Relations* on Mackenzie's reputation on pages 370-72 of his study.

5. This dust-jacket laudation of *Poor Relations* came with the new edition of the novel published in London by Macdonald in 1949.

6. *Poor Relations* (London, 1919), p. 77.

7. Katherine Mansfield's review appeared in *The Athenaeum*, October 17, 1919; reprinted in *Novels and Novelists*, ed. J. Middleton Murry (London, 1930), pp. 88-90.

8. See Waugh's review, which is quoted and discussed in Erlandson, pp. 371-72.

9. *New Statesman*, Sept. 27, 1919, p. 656. Quoted in Erlandson, p. 372.

10. Review of *Rich Relatives* by E. S. (Edward Shanks) in *London Mercury*, IV (1921), 545.

11. *Rich Relatives* (London, 1921), p. 58.

12. *Ibid.*, p. 31.

13. Edward Shanks, *op. cit.;* Kenneth Young, *Compton Mackenzie*, pp. 19-20.

14. Octave VI, p. 63.

15. Octave V, p. 153.

16. *The Letters of F. Scott Fitzgerald*, p. 356.

17. Octave VI, p. 12.

18. Octave V, p. 247; foreword to the new edition of the novel published under the title *Paradise for Sale* (London, 1963).

19. Foreword to *Paradise for Sale.*

20. *Paradise for Sale*, p. 247.

21. Octave V, pp. 225 ff.

22. *Extremes Meet*, Four Square Edition (London, 1966 [1928]), p. 245.

23. *Vestal Fire* (London, 1927), p. 47.

24. V. S. Pritchett, "Norman Douglas: 1868-1952," *New Statesman and Nation*, XLIII (1952), 307.

25. Octave VI, p. 93.

26. Octave VI, p. 94.

27. *Vestal Fire*, p. 37.

28. *Ibid.*, p. 5.

29. *Ibid.*, pp. 132-33.

30. *Ibid.*, p. 28.

31. Octave VI, p. 106.

32. *Ibid.*, p. 118.

33. *Ibid.*, p. 148.

34. *Ibid.*

35. Kathleen Nott, "Girls Will Be Boys," *Observer,* September 15, 1968, p. 29 — review of a paperback edition of *The Well of Loneliness* together with Vera Brittain's *Radclyffe Hall: A Case of Obscenity.*

36. Jeannette H. Foster, *Sex Variant Women in Literature* (London, 1958), pp. 281-82.

37. Octave VI, p. 118.

38. Leo Robertson, *Compton Mackenzie,* p. 125.

39. See chapter 9 of *Zuleika Dobson.*

40. *Extraordinary Women* (London, 1928), p. 121.

Chapter Six

1. Octave VI, p. 171.

2. Octave VII, p. 60.

3. *Ibid.*

4. Octave VII, p. 233.

5. Octave VII, p. 204.

6. Quoted in a dust-jacket blurb of *The East Wind;* I have not checked the original.

7. Also quoted on a dust-jacket; this is presumably the review, by Douglas West, to which Mackenzie refers in Octave VIII, p. 218.

8. Leo Robertson, *Compton Mackenzie,* p. 223.

9. Kenneth Young, *Compton Mackenzie,* p. 21.

10. Derek Traversi, review of *West to North, The Tablet,* Nov. 23, 1940, p. 413.

11. Cuthbert Wright, review of *Again to the North* (American title of the second volume of *The North Wind of Love),* *Commonweal,* LXIV (June 28, 1946), 267-68.

12. Octave V, "Apologia."

13. *The East Wind of Love* (London, 1937), p. 499.

14. *Ibid.,* p. 529.

15. *Ibid.,* p. 555.

16. *The South Wind of Love* (London, 1937), p. 482. This passage, from a letter, is in italics in the original.

17. *Ibid.,* p. 661.

18. *Ibid.,* p. 804.

19. *The West Wind of Love* (London, 1940), p. 269.

20. Said in a lecture on "Writers I Have Known" before the Royal Society of Literature in London on April 20, 1967.

21. *The North Wind of Love* (London, 1944), p. 70.

22. *Ibid.,* p. 151. A Nationalist party, with a policy of complete independence from England, was founded in Scotland in 1928. It took about forty years for it to amount to a significant political force; in 1968 it claimed to have a hundred thousand members. See David Holden, "Nationalism is No Joke Now," London *Sunday Times,* April 21, 1968, p. 13. There are

numerous books on the subject, including H. J. Paton, *The Claim of Scotland* (London, 1968).

23. E. M. Forster, *Howards End* (New York, 1954), pp. 29-30.

24. J. M. Synge, Preface to *The Playboy of the Western World, The Plays and Poems of J. M. Synge,* ed. T. R. Henn (London, 1963), pp. 174-75.

25. *The East Wind of Love,* p. 513.

26. *The North Wind of Love, II* (London, 1945), p. 167.

27. Robertson, *Compton Mackenzie,* pp. 167-68.

28. *The East Wind of Love,* p. 250.

29. Cyril Connolly, "Mr. Mossbross Takes the Stand," *The Condemned Playground* (London, 1945), pp. 106-07.

30. *The North Wind of Love,* p. 138.

31. Young, *Compton Mackenzie,* pp. 22-23.

32. Derek Traversi, *op. cit.*

Chapter Seven

1. The story of the trial is told in Octave VII, pp. 83-103. Sir Reginald Poole's remarks are on p. 94.

2. *The Times,* January 13, 1933, p. 13.

3. *Water on the Brain* (London, 1933), p. 85.

4. London *Sunday Times,* October 8, 1967, pp. 21-25 and 35; October 15, pp. 21-23; October 22, pp. 45-47. Mackenzie's "Colonel V" is mentioned on p. 24 of the first article.

5. Octave VIII, p. 96.

6. *The Red Tapeworm* (London, 1941), p. 1.

7. *Ibid.,* p. 143.

8. *Ibid.,* p. 15.

9. *The Lunatic Republic* (London, 1959), p. 77.

10. Y. M. Biese, is his *Notes on the Vocabulary in Compton Mackenzie's Novel The Lunatic Republic* (Turku, 1963), makes this general comment. Biese has found about 250 words which Mackenzie coined for his Lunatic-Basic variety of English; besides emphasizing that the language is not designed for humorous purposes only, Biese brings to light the care and ingenuity which Mackenzie employed in constructing it.

11. *The Lunatic Republic,* p. 145.

12. *Mezzotint* (London, 1961), p. 182.

Chapter Eight

1. Octave VI, p. 138.

2. *Ibid.,* p. 160.

3. Octave VII, pp. 189-193.

4. *The Red Tapeworm,* p. 147.

5. Mackenzie made this statement in a talk we had on April 19, 1967. In Octave VIII, pages 218-19, he quotes a letter from Cameron of Lochiel complimenting him on *The Monarch of the Glen* and *Keep the Home Guard*

Turning, and saying, "Ben Nevis is a great character." *A propos* of the letter, Mackenzie writes, "After *The Monarch of the Glen* was published people in the North were continually saying it was a portrait of Cameron of Lochiel. As I had never had Lochiel in my mind when I was writing the book this used to annoy me. Ben Nevis was a character created entirely by imagination."

6. Octave VIII, p. 135. "However, in spite of the temporary hold-up," Mackenzie continues, *"The Monarch of the Glen* became a steady seller and is still in print a quarter of a century later."

7. *The Monarch of the Glen* (London, 1941), p. 22.

8. *Ibid.,* p. 64.

9. *Ibid.,* p. 14.

10. Leo Robertson, *Compton Mackenzie,* pp. 140-41.

11. Letter quoted in Octave VIII, p. 252.

12. From a newspaper account quoted in Octave VII, p. 173.

13. *Keep the Home Guard Turning* (London, 1943), p. 202.

14. Foreword to Arthur Swinson, *Scotch on the Rocks* (London, 1963), pp. 10-11.

15. *Ibid.,* p. 187.

16. *Whisky Galore* (London, 1951 [1947]), p. 18.

17. *Ibid.,* pp. 133-34.

18. "Rocket Range Protest/Sir C. Mackenzie's Call to Crofters," London *Times,* August 17, 1955, p. 4. See also the issues of August 22, p. 4; August 26, p. 7; September 20, p. 9; and September 30, p. 9. That the issue was not soon forgotten is shown by a story in the *Times,* August 11, 1969, p. 6, entitled "Furious Battle of Lobsters and Rockets." The rocket range on South Uist had put some of the richest lobster grounds out of use, and at a protest meeting the fishermen responded in the manner Mackenzie described. After nearly three hours of confused oratory, "a hirsute, kilted, bearded Goliath, who looked as if he used a sabre as a toothpick," led his militant followers out of the meeting in disgust. So the war goes on.

19. *Rockets Galore* (London, 1957), pp. 77-78.

20. *Ibid.,* p. 107.

21. *Ibid.,* pp. 84-85.

Chapter Nine

1. Preface to *Gallipoli Memories* (London, 1929), p. x.

2. Letter of Faith Compton Mackenzie to Mackenzie's mother, March 8, 1929, quoted in Octave VI, p. 177.

3. *Gallipoli Memories,* p. 2.

4. *Ibid.,* pp. 7-8. The letter is dated March 23, 1915.

5. *Ibid.,* pp. 181-82.

6. *Ibid.,* pp. 80-81.

7. *Ibid.,* p. 124.

8. *Ibid.,* pp. 373-74.

9. *Aegean Memories* (London, 1940), p. 91.

10. Octave VII, p. 87.

11. *The Times,* March 31, 1931, p. 20.

12. *Aegean Memories,* p. 234.

13. *Ibid.,* p. 182.

14. Octave VII, p. 119.

15. Kenneth Young, *Compton Mackenzie,* p. 23.

16. Cyril Connolly, "Mr. Mossbross Takes the Class," in *The Condemned Playground* (London, 1945), pp. 106-107; Young, p. 23.

17. Compton Mackenzie, *Literature in My Time* (London, 1933), pp. 193-98.

18. *Ibid.,* p. 203.

19. *Ibid.,* p. 210-11.

20. "Prologue and Apologia," Octave I, p. 13.

21. *Ibid.,* p. 16.

22. *Ibid.,* p. 15.

23. John Bowen, review of Octave III, London *Sunday Times,* October 4, 1964, p. 48.

24. Sir Charles Petrie, review of Octave I, *Illustrated London News,* January 26, 1963, p. 117.

25. A. P. Ryan, review of Octave VIII, London *Times,* February 1, 1969, p. 23.

26. E. C. Beer, review of Octave III, Toronto *Globe Magazine,* January 20, 1965, p. 13.

27. H. D. Ziman, review of Octave VI, London *Daily Telegraph,* February 23, 1967, p. 20.

28. "Prologue and Apologia," Octave I, 13.

29. Octave VIII, p. 138.

30. "Sir Compton Mackenzie 'Face to Face,' " *Listener,* January 25, 1962, pp. 165-67.

31. My wife and I asked Mackenzie about a man named Wynne Davies, the brother of a neighbor of ours. He remembered him from his days in Cornwall, knew that he had later gone to Nigeria, and also recalled that he had come from Oswestry in Wales. This we judged a pretty fair feat of memory, since Mackenzie was recalling events of sixty years before.

32. Octave VI, p. 131. He told the same story in his Tredegar Memorial Lecture on "Writers I Have Known" before the Royal Society of Literature on April 20, 1967.

33. Hugo Williams, review of Octave VII, *Listener,* July 11, 1968, p. 54.

34. John Bowen, *op. cit.*

35. Kenneth Young, Compton Mackenzie, p. 27.

36. Octave VII, p. 132.

37. Peter Dickinson, review of Octave V, *Punch,* March 16, 1966, p. 399.

38. Review of Octave I, *Times Literary Supplement,* January 18, 1963, p. 35.

39. Walter Allen, "London Letter," *New York Times Book Review,* March 3, 1968, p. 20.

40. John Raymond, review of Octave I, London *Sunday Times,* January 20, 1963, p. 31.

41. Review of Octave II, *T.L.S.,* October 11, 1963, p. 802.

42. E. C. Beer, *op. cit.*

43. Charles Curran, review of Octave VIII, London *Sunday Telegraph,* February 2, 1969, p. 10.

44. Robert Speaight, review of Octave IV, *The Tablet,* July 17, 1965, p. 800.

45. John Raymond, review of Octave I, London *Sunday Times,* January 20, 1963, p. 31, and of Octave IV, June 27, 1965, p. 41.

46. David Hughes, review of Octave II, London *Sunday Times, October 13, 1963, p. 37.*

47. Review of Octave VIII, *T.L.S.,* February 6, 1969, p. 131.

48. Auberon Waugh, review of Octave VII, *Spectator,* March 1, 1968, p. 270.

49. Raymond Mortimer, review of Octave VII, London *Sunday Times,* January 21, 1968, p. 51.

Chapter Ten

1. Compton Mackenzie, *Greece in My Life* (London, 1960), p. 16.

2. Octave I, p. 189.

3. *Catholicism and Scotland* (London, 1936), p. 84.

4. *Ibid.,* p. 1.

5. Review of *Catholicism and Scotland* by "G.M.," *Blackfriars,* XVII (1936), 395.

6. *Marathon and Salamis* (London, 1934), pp. 154-55.

7. See Octave VIII, p. 194.

8. *Mr. Roosevelt* (London, 1943), p. 245.

9. *Dr. Benes* (London, 1946), p. 33.

10. *Ibid.,* p. 269.

11. Angus Wilson, "Broken Promise," *The Listener,* April 12, 1951, pp. 575-76.

12. Katherine Fullerton Gerould, "British Novelists, Ltd.," *Yale Review,* n. s. VII (1918), 161-85, especially pp. 161, 169, and 184.

13. P. P. Howe, "Fiction and Perpetual Life," *The Athenaeum,* June 6, 1919, pp. 422-23.

14. James E. Miller, Jr., *The Fictional Technique of Scott Fitzgerald* (The Hague, 1957), p. 17.

15. See Henry James, "The Younger Generation," *T.L.S.,* March 19 and April 2, 1914, pp. 133-34 and 137-58, reprinted in Leon Edel and Gordon N. Ray, eds., *Henry James and H. G. Wells* (London, 1959), pp. 178-215.

16. *Ibid.,* p. 186.

17. *Ibid.*

18. G. S. Fraser, *The Modern Writer and his World* (Harmondsworth, 1964), pp. 105-06.

19. Gordon Hall Gerould, *The Patterns of English and American Fiction* (Boston, 1942), p. 485.

20. Edmund Wilson, "On British Writers," London *Sunday Times,* September 2, 1962, p. 21.

21. This address is printed as Appendix B of Octave VII, pp. 293-304.

Selected Bibliography

PRIMARY SOURCES

1. Novels:

The Passionate Elopement. London: Secker, 1911.
Carnival. London: Secker, 1912.
Sinister Street. 2 Vols. London: Secker, 1913-1914.
Guy and Pauline. London: Secker, 1915.
The Early Life and Adventures of Sylvia Scarlett. London: Secker, 1918.
Sylvia & Michael. London: Secker, 1919.
Poor Relations. London: Secker, 1919.
The Vanity Girl. London: Cassell, 1920.
Rich Relatives. London: Secker, 1921.
The Altar Steps. First volume of religious trilogy. London: Cassell, 1922.
The Seven Ages of Woman. London: Secker, 1923.
The Parson's Progress. Second volume of religious trilogy. London: Cassell, 1923.
The Heavenly Ladder. Third volume of religious trilogy. London: Cassell, 1924.
The Old Men of the Sea. London: Cassell, 1924.
Coral. London: Cassell, 1925.
Fairy Gold. London: Cassell, 1926.
Rogues and Vagabonds. London: Cassell, 1927.
Vestal Fire. London: Cassell, 1927.
Extremes Meet. London: Cassell, 1928.
Extraordinary Women. Themes and Variations. London: Secker, 1928.
The Three Couriers. London: Cassell, 1929.
April Fools. A farce of manners. London: Cassell, 1930.
Our Street. London: Cassell, 1931.
Water on the Brain. London: Cassell, 1933.
The Darkening Green. London: Cassell, 1934.
Figure of Eight. London: Cassell, 1936.
The Four Winds of Love, 6 Vols. (1937-45): *The East Wind,* 1937; *The South Wind,* 1937; *The West Wind,* 1940; *West to North,* 1940; *The North Wind,* Vol. I, 1944; *The North Wind,* Vol. II, 1945. Re-

published in eight volumes, 1949. The first two volumes were published
by Rich and Cowan; the remainder by Chatto and Windus.
The Red Tapeworm. London: Chatto and Windus, 1941.
The Monarch of the Glen. London: Chatto and Windus, 1941.
Keep the Home Guard Turning. London: Chatto and Windus, 1943.
Whisky Galore. London: Chatto and Windus, 1947.
Hunting the Fairies. London: Chatto and Windus, 1949.
The Rival Monster. London: Chatto and Windus, 1952.
Ben Nevis Goes East. London: Chatto and Windus, 1954.
Thin Ice. London: Chatto and Windus, 1956.
Rockets Galore. London: Chatto and Windus, 1957.
The Lunatic Republic. London: Chatto and Windus, 1959.
Mezzotint. London: Chatto and Windus, 1961.
The Stolen Soprano. London: Chatto and Windus, 1965.
Paper Lives. London: Chatto and Windus, 1966.

2. Selected List of Other Works:

Gallipoli Memories. London: Cassell, 1929.
First Athenian Memories. London: Cassell, 1931.
Greek Memories. London: Cassell, 1932.
Unconsidered Trifles. A collection of essays. London: Secker, 1932.
Literature in My Time. London: Rich and Cowan, 1933.
Reaped and Bound. A collection of essays. London: Secker, 1933.
Prince Charlie and his Ladies. London: Cassell, 1934.
Marathon and Salamis. London: Peter Davies, 1934.
Catholicism and Scotland. London: Routledge, 1936.
Pericles. London: Hodder and Stoughton, 1937.
The Windsor Tapestry. London: Rich and Cowan, 1938.
A Musical Chair: Editorials from The Gramophone. London: Chatto and
    Windus, 1939.
Aegean Memories. London: Chatto and Windus, 1940.
Wind of Freedom. The Invasion of Greece, 1940-41. London: Chatto and
    Windus, 1943.
Mr. Roosevelt. London: Harrap, 1943.
Dr. Benes. London: Harrap, 1946.
All over the Place. London: Chatto and Windus, 1949.
Eastern Epic. The Indian Army in the Second World War.
Echoes. Broadcast talks. London: Chatto and Windus, 1954.
Sublime Tobacco. London: Chatto and Windus, 1957.
Greece in My Life. London: Chatto and Windus, 1960.
On Moral Courage. London: Collins, 1962.
My Life and Times. Ten volumes. London: Chatto and Windus, 1963-1971.

SECONDARY SOURCES

ADCOCK, A. ST. JOHN. *Gods of Modern Grub Street.* London: Sampson Low, Marston, 1923. Truer psychology in Mackenzie's novels than in those of Freudians.

BRION, MARCEL. "Compton Mackenzie." *Le Monde,* October 4, 1950, 8. A pure Celt, living his fantasies as well as writing them.

CUNLIFFE, J.W. *English Literature during the Last Half Century.* 2nd ed. New York: Macmillan, 1923. Mackenzie one of four "new novelists" given detailed treatment; sees him sometimes betrayed by his versatility and love of detail.

EDEL, LEON. and RAY, GORDON N., eds. *Henry James and H.G. Wells: A Record of their Friendship, their Debate on the Art of Fiction, and their Quarrel.* London: Rupert Hart-Davis, 1958. Contains Henry James's "The Younger Generation," describing Mackenzie as perhaps the most promising of the younger novelists.

ELIOT T.S. "London Letter." *The Dial,* LXXIII (September, 1922), 329-331. Mackenzie better worth reading than many more pretentious and sophisticated writers.

ERLANDSON, THEODORE ROY. "A Critical Study of Some Early Novels (1911-1920) of Sir Compton Mackenzie." Unpublished dissertation, University of Southern California, 1965. Excellent analysis of the rise and fall of his reputation.

FREEMAN, JOHN. *English Portraits and Essays.* London: Hodder and Stoughton, 1924. What is the secret of Mackenzie's failure? He has not concerned himself with life except in its externals. But his instability makes expectation foolish.

———. "The Novels of Mr. Compton Mackenzie." *London Mercury,* I (February 1920), 448-57. Conspicuous gifts, but has chosen the easier way.

GEORGE, W.L. *A Novelist on Novels.* London: Collins, 1918. Mackenzie as one of nine possible successors to Wells, Bennett, and Galsworthy; but needs to exercise restraint.

GEROULD, KATHARINE FULLERTON. "British Novelists, Ltd." *Yale Review,* n. s. VII (October, 1917), 161-85; The British novelists sound so alike they must all be members of the same syndicate.

GOLDRING, DOUGLAS. *Reputations: Essays in Criticism.* New York: Thomas Seltzer, 1920. Mackenzie has found his niche as an entertainer.

GOULD, GERALD. *The English Novel of Today.* London: John Castle, 1924. Mackenzie did not invent the quasi-biographical novel, but established its vogue.

GUEDALLA, PHILIP. *A Gallery.* London: Constable, 1924. Amusing satire of Mackenzie and *Sinister Street.*

HOLLIS, CHRISTOPHER. "Compton Mackenzie Remembered." *Tablet,* CCXXVI (December 9, 1972), 1175.

HOLLOWAY, DAVID. "Sir Compton Mackenzie, Man of Many Words, Dies at 89." *Daily Telegraph* (London), December 1, 1972, p. 6.

JOHNSON, R. BRIMLEY. *Some Contemporary Novelists (Men)*. London: Leonard Parsons, 1922. Romantic; innocent of moral intention.

JORDAN, PHILIP. "Compton Mackenzie's Blind Spot." *Everyman*, VII (June 9, 1932), 626. Too good an entertainer for the public to take him seriously.

KENNEDY, MARGARET. *The Outlaws on Parnassus*. London: Cresset Press, 1958. Shrewd comments on the writing of novels, with Mackenzie as example of a writer who uses a mask: in the novels he does not give himself away at all.

LAWRENCE, D.H. *Collected Letters*. Ed. Harry T. Moore. London: Heinemann, 1962. Capri, 1920, Lawrence's double view of Mackenzie and *The Man Who Loved Islands*.

LINKLATER, ERIC. *Edinburgh*. Cities of Enchantment Series. London: Newnes, 1960. Mackenzie as Edinburgh personality.

———. *The Man on My Back: An Autobiography*. New York: Macmillan, 1941. Memoirs of a friend of long standing.

LOCKHART, SIR ROBERT BRUCE. *Friends, Foes, and Foreigners*. London: Putman, 1957. Memoir by a British diplomat and intelligence agent, containing a chapter on Mackenzie, "our Scottish Cyrano de Bergerac," describing his life in Edinburgh.

MACKENZIE, FAITH COMPTON. *Always Afternoon*. London: Collins, 1943.

———. *As Much as I Dare*. London: Collins, 1938.

———. *More than I Should*. London: Collins, 1940.

Reveal a very unusual marriage, in which each went his own way.

MAIS, S.P.B. *Books and their Writers*. London: Grant Richards, 1920. High praise for "our vicarious adventurer."

MANSFIELD, KATHERINE. *Novels and Novelists*. New York: Knopf, 1930. Reviews favorable and unfavorable.

McLAREN, MORAY. *Compton Mackenzie: A Panegyric for his Eightieth Birthday*. Edinburgh: M. MacDonald, 1963. Delivered at the Scottish Arts Club in Edinburgh, at a birthday celebration.

MILLER, JAMES E., JR. *The Fictional Technique of Scott Fitzgerald*. The Hague: Martinus Nijhoff, 1957. Fitzgerald's turning from the novel of saturation (influenced by Mackenzie) to the novel of selection.

NICHOLS, BEVERLY. *Twenty-five*. London: Cape, 1926. Legends he has heard of Mackenzie's exploits in Athens in wartime.

PROCTOR, MORTIMER R. *The English University Novel*. Berkeley: University of California Press, 1957. Excellent discussion of *Sinister Street;* regards it as the best of its kind.

RAYMOND, JOHN. "Books in General." *New Statesman and Nation*, XLVIII (Dec. 25, 1954), 860-61. Extraordinary actor's quality about his writing; an ageless and indestructible *farceur*.

ROBERTSON, LEO. *Compton Mackenzie*. London: Richards, 1954. Shrewd insights occasionally, but a fellow clubman's book; laudatory rather than critical.

"Sir Compton Mackenzie 'Face to Face.' " *The Listener,* LXVII (January 25, 1962), 165-67. Television interview in which John Freeman pressed him hard about accuracy of memory and literary achievement.

STRONG, L.A.G. "Books and Writers." *Spectator,* CLXXXVII (September 14, 1951), 1-4. Stresses inventiveness, comic skill, and ability to evoke the past.

SWINNERTON, FRANK. *Background with Chorus.* London: Hutchinson, 1956. Excellent portrait of Mackenzie.

———. *Figures in the Foreground.* London: Hutchinson, 1963. Deals especially with Mackenzie's relations with an old rival, Hugh Walpole.

———. *The Georgian Literary Scene.* Rev. Ed. London: Dent, 1951. Vividness of mimicry; has not plumbed the depths of his talents.

———. *Swinnerton: An Autobiography.* New York: Doubleday, Doran, 1936. Mackenzie's incorrigible Romanticism; greater as a personality than as a writer.

TAYLOR, WILFRID. *Scot Free.* London: Max Reinhardt, 1953. Incidental reminiscences; vivid account of Mackenzie reading a film script of *The Monarch of the Glen* and acting out all the parts himself.

WAUGH, ARTHUR. *Tradition and Change: Studies in Contemporary Literature,* 2nd ed. London: Chapman and Hall, 1919. Includes Mackenzie in a chapter on "The New Realism."

WEINER, JOYCE. "Seventy Happy Years." *John o'London's Weekly,* LXII (January 23, 1953). Mackenzie's vitality in life and as chronicler of the human comedy.

WILSON, ANGUS. "Broken Promise." *Listener,* April 12, 1951, pp. 575-576. Failure of the younger novelists of 1914 to fulfill their early promise.

WILSON, EDMUND. *The Bit between my Teeth.* London: W. H. Allan, 1965. Asserts that Mackenzie is a vastly underrated novelist.

WOOLF, VIRGINIA. *Contemporary Writers.* London: Hogarth Press, 1965. Reviews of Sylvia Scarlett novels.

YOUNG, JESSICA BRETT. *Francis Brett Young: A Biography.* London: Heinemann, 1962. Mackenzie in the Capri period, by the widow of a great friend and fellow novelist.

YOUNG, KENNETH. *Compton Mackenzie.* Writers and their Work Series. London: Longmans, Green, 1968. Witty reassessment; concludes that at least half a dozen of his novels will last.

Index